Saint Luke of Simferopol
(Prince Yasenetsky-Voino)

I CAME TO LOVE SUFFERING
AUTOBIOGRAPHY

Gozalov Books Publishing
The Hague

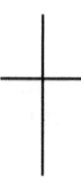

This book has the blessing of
Monsignor Simon,
Archbishop of Brussels and Belgium

© Gozalov Books Publishing, The Hague, 2022
Tel.: +31 (0)70 352 15 65
E-mail: gozalovbooks@planet.nl
Website: www.hetsmallepad.nl

Second edition
ISBN: 9789079889631; 978-90-79889-63-1

Editor: Convent of the Mother of God Portaïtissa, Trazegnies, Belgium, portaitissa@skynet.be
Translation: Gozalov Books
Proofreading: Frits Bot
Design: Guram Kochi and Marijcke Tooneman

All rights reserved. No part of this publication may be reproduced or transmitted in any form or by any means, electronic or mechanical, including photocopy and recording, or stored in a retrieval system, without the written permission of the publisher.

Table of Contents

Foreword from the publishers 5
Chapter 1. Youth 9
Chapter 2. Work in country hospitals 14
Chapter 3. Priesthood 24
Chapter 4. First exile 34
Chapter 5. Before the second exile 49
Chapter 6. Exile to Archangelsk 57
Chapter 7. Third arrest 65
Appendices 71
Eindnotes 76

FOREWORD FROM THE PUBLISHERS

The author of this book, Saint Luke the Confessor (his worldly name was Valentin Yasenetsky-Voyno), is a Russian saint of the twentieth century. He was born on April 27, 1877 in Kerch, Crimea and fell asleep in the Lord on June 11, 1961 in Simferopol, Crimea. Canonized by the Ukrainian Orthodox Church (Moscow Patriarchate) in November 1995.

He was a descendent of a Belarusian-Polish impoverished princely family, and he was archbishop of the Russian Orthodox Church and at the same time a prominent physician, surgeon, inventor, scientist, writer and painter.

The title of this book is a quote from Saint Luke's letter to his eldest son Mikhail. The full sentence is: "I began to love suffering that so amazingly purifies the soul."

From an early age, his ideal was to serve the needy and sick, and so he abandoned his successful study at the Art Academy and graduated as a doctor from the University of Kiev. To everyone's surprise, he said, "I studied medicine with one goal in mind: to work my whole life in the province as a doctor for the peasants." Indeed, he worked for several years under very unfavourable conditions as a general practitioner and surgeon in the remote towns and villages of Russia and the Ukraine, saving lives and performing spectacular operations, especially on the eyes. During the Russian Japanese war he worked in a military hospital. At the same time, he did scientific investigation of some cases from his practice, and learned several European languages to study Western professional literature.

His innovative ideas and advanced surgical techniques received wide recognition in the Russian as well as the European medical world. He became head of the chair of surgery at several institutes and was honoured with a number of scientific titles. He received awards for some of his medical scientific works.

He inherited the deep religiosity of his father, and from an early age he became known for his spontaneous public sermons on the Christian way and values.

During the severe trials of the Russian Church, when the communists had come to power in the country and were engaged in a methodical genocide of the clergy, Innocenty, Bishop of Tashkent, asked him to become a priest. Valentin Yasenetsky accepted this request and received priestly ordination, with the bishop describing his future mission in the words of the Holy Apostle Paul: "not to baptize, but to evangelize." (1Cor 1:17)

Over the years, after the death of his beloved wife, he took monastic vows and was named after the holy Evangelist Luke; then he was ordained a bishop. After many prosecutions by the Soviet authorities and convictions on false grounds (including false testimonials from some colleagues, students and friends, as well as false reports, elicited by the secret police) and an exile for many years to Siberia, above the Arctic Circle, he was eventually released and he ended his days as Archbishop of Simferopol and Crimea. Throughout all the trials, he remained true to his Russian Orthodox faith and principles, and continued his work as a doctor and scientist, despite the blindness that struck him in the last years of his life. Our special thanks to Archimandrite Nikon (Yakimov), Rector of the Russian Orthodox Church of Saint Mary Magdalene in The Hague, who brought this amazing book to our attention.

Marijcke Tooneman and Guram Kochi, Gozalov Books Publishing

The Hague, January 2021

Saint Luke the Confessor

"The body is composed of not only many, but also unequal parts, which are in turn composed of four elements. When it falls ill, it is in need of various medicines and, moreover, medicine composed of various herbs. The soul, on the contrary, is immaterial, and therefore simple and uncomplicated. When ill, one medicine heals it: the holy Spirit, the grace of the Lord Jesus Christ."

Venerable Symeon the New Theologian

"O mother of mine, desecrated, despised mother, holy church of Christ! You shone with the light of truth and love, and now, what is the matter? Thousands and thousands of churches across the face of the Russian land are ruined and destroyed, while others are profaned, and still others turned into vegetable storehouses, populated by nonbelievers, and only a few are preserved. In the place of beautiful cathedrals: smoothly paved empty squares or theaters and cinemas. O mother of mine, holy church! Who is guilty of your desecration? Only the builders of the new life, of the church of the earthly kingdom, of equality, social justice and abundance of the fruits of the earth? No, we must say with bitter tears, not only they, but the people themselves. With what tears will our people pay, our people who have forgotten the way to the church of God?"

Archbishop Luke (Voyno-Yasenetsky)[1]

Chapter 1. Youth

My father was catholic, very devout, he always went to church and prayed at home for hours. Father was a man of remarkably pure soul, in no one did he see anything wrong, and he trusted everybody, although he was surrounded by dishonest people because of his profession. In our orthodox family, he, as a catholic, was somewhat alienated.

Mother prayed at home fervently, but she never went to church, it seems. The reason of this was her indignation about the greed and quarrels of the priests that were going on before her eyes. My two brothers, lawyers, did not show signs of religiosity. However, they always went to the placing in the tomb[2] and kissed the shroud, and they always were at the Easter morning service. When she was a student, my older sister was shaken with horror by the accident at Khodynka Field. She developed a mental illness, and jumped out of a window from the third floor. She had severe hip and shoulder fractures and kidney ruptures. Subsequently she developed kidney stones from which she died, having lived only twenty-five years. My younger sister is well up to now. She is a beautiful and very pious woman.

I did not receive a religious education in the family, and if it is possible to talk about hereditary religiosity at all, then probably I inherited it mainly from my very devout father. Since childhood I had a passion for drawing, and I graduated simultaneously from the gymnasium and the Kiev art school, where I showed considerable artistic abilities. I participated in a travelling exhibition with a small picture of a beggarly old man, standing with a hand stretched out. My attraction to painting was so strong that when I finished gymnasium I decided to go to the Saint Petersburg academy of arts.

But during the entrance examinations I suffered heavy doubts about whether I had chosen the correct path in life. A brief period of hesitation ended by deciding that I had no right to study what I like, but that I was obliged to study what is useful for suffering people. From the academy I sent a telegram to my mother about my desire to enter medical school. However, all places had already been taken. I was offered to enter the faculty of natural sciences, in order to switch to medicine afterwards. I refused because I had a great dislike of natural sciences. I did have a pronounced interest in the humanities, particularly in theology, philosophy and history. So I preferred to go to the faculty of law. I spent a year studying with interest history and philosophy of law, political economy, and Roman law.

But a year later I was again overwhelmingly attracted to painting. I set off for Munich, where I entered the private art school of professor Knirr. However, already after three weeks I was drawn home irrepressibly by homesickness. I went to Kiev and for a year I intensely studied drawing and painting with a group of friends.

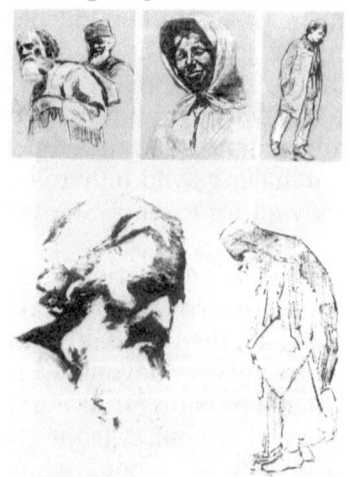

At this time my faith showed its first signs. Every day, and sometimes twice a day, I went to the Kiev Lavra of the Caves. I was often in the Kiev churches and when I returned from there, I would sketch what I had seen in the lavra and the churches. I did a lot of drawings, sketches and drafts of praying people and of pilgrims who had travelled to the lavra for a thousand versts. Then already the direction of artistic activity took form, in which I would have worked if I had not left painting. I would have gone the road of Vasnetsov[3] and Nesterov[4], for the principal religious direction in my pursuit of painting was already clearly defined. By this time I clearly understood the process of artistic creation. Everywhere, on the streets and in trams, on squares and in bazaars, I observed all pronounced facial features, shapes, movements, and upon returning home I sketched all this. At the exhibition of the Kiev art school I received an award for these sketches of mine.

To rest from this work I walked every day for two versts along the bank of the Dnieper; on the road I was thinking hard about very difficult theological and philosophical questions. Nothing of course, came out of these thoughts of mine, because I had no scientific training.

At the same time I became passionately engrossed in the ethical teaching of Leo Tolstoy[5] and became, one might say, a confirmed Tolstoyan: I slept on the floor on a carpet and in the summer when I was at the dacha I mowed grass and rye along with the peasants without lagging behind them. However, my Tolstoyism did not last long, only until the time when I read his essay "What I believe."[6] His essay was published abroad because it was banned. It repulsed me strongly by its mockery of the orthodox faith. I immediately realized that Tolstoy was a heretic, very far from true Christianity.

Not long before that I had painstakingly read the New Testament which had given me a correct idea of the teaching of Christ. According to good old custom I had received the holy book from the headmaster when I was handed the school-leaving certificate as a farewell gift for life. I kept this holy book for decades. Very many passages in it made a deep impression on me. I marked them with a red pencil.

But nothing could compare with the tremendous power of the impression that was produced by the passage of the Gospel in which Jesus shows the disciples the fields of ripe wheat, and says to them: "The harvest truly is plenteous, but the labourers are few. Pray ye therefore the Lord of the harvest, that He will send forth labourers' into His harvest."[7] My heart literally trembled, I silently said, "O Lord! Do You really have too few labourers?!" Later, after many years, when the Lord called me to be a worker on His grain field, I was sure that this evangelical text was the first time God called me to serve Him.

This rather strange year went by like that. It was possible to enroll at the medical faculty, but again I was overwhelmed by doubts of populist nature. According to my youthful impulsiveness, I decided I needed as soon as possible to take up useful practical work for the common people. My thoughts were roaming about becoming a medical assistant or a country school teacher, and in this mood I once went to the director of the public colleges in the Kiev school district with the request to place me in one of the schools. The director turned out to be a sensible man with an astute mind. He appreciated my populist aspirations, but very energetically discouraged me from what I was planning, and persuaded me to enter the medical faculty.

This was consistent with my desire to be useful to farmers whose medical aid was so badly provided for, but my near aversion of natural sciences stood in the way. Nevertheless I overcame this aversion and entered the medical faculty at the university of Kiev.

When I studied physics, chemistry, mineralogy, I had the almost physical sensation that I was forcing my brain to work on what was alien to it. My brain, like a squeezed rubber ball, tried to push out contents foreign to it. Nonetheless, I got only excellent marks and unexpectedly I became very interested in anatomy. I investigated bones. At home I drew and sculpted them from clay. And with my dissection of corpses I immediately attracted the attention of all the fellow students and the professor of anatomy. Already in the second year my fellow students unanimously decided that I would be a professor of anatomy, and their prophecy came true. After twenty years I really did become a professor of topographic anatomy and operative surgery.

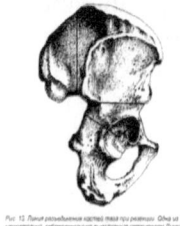 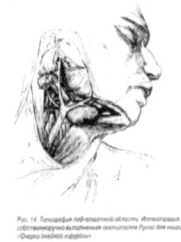

In the third year I became passionately interested in studying operations on dead bodies. My capabilities underwent an interesting evolution: my love for form turned into love of anatomy and my ability to draw subtly turned into precise artful skill when doing anatomical dissection and during operations on dead bodies. From a failed painter, I became an artist in anatomy and surgery.

In the third year, I was unexpectedly elected class representative. It happened like this: before one lecture I learned that one of my fellow students on the course, a Pole, struck another fellow student, a Jew, on the cheek. At the end of the lecture, I stood up and asked for attention. All fell silent. I made a passionate speech in which I denounced the disgraceful act of the Polish student. I talked about lofty standards of morality, about projection of resentment, I called to mind the great Socrates, who reacted calmly to his quarrelsome wife when she poured a pot of dirty water over his head. This speech made such a great impression that I was unanimously elected class representative.

I passed the state exams brilliantly with only excellent marks. The professor of general surgery told me at the exam: "Doctor, you now know a lot more than I do, because you already know all parts of medicine, and I have forgotten a lot that does not apply directly to my specialty."

Only for the exam in medicinal chemistry[8] I got three out of five. For the theoretical exam I did excellently, but I still had to do a urinalysis. As it was regrettably the custom, the laboratory assistant took money from the students in exchange for telling what should be found in the first flask and in the test tube, so I knew that in the urine I was given to explore there was sugar. However, due to a small mistake Trommer's reaction did not happen, and when the professor, without looking at me asked, "Well, what did you find there? " I could have said that I had found sugar, but I said Trommer's reaction did not reveal sugar.

This one 'three' mark did not prevent me to get a physician's degree with honours.

When we all got our diplomas, my course mates asked me what occupation I intended to have. When I replied that I intended to be a country doctor, they opened their eyes wide and said: "What, you will be a country doctor?! Why, you are a scientist by vocation!" I was offended by the fact they did not understand me, because I studied medicine with the sole purpose of being my whole life long a rural peasant doctor to help poor people.[9]

Chapter 2. Work in country hospitals

I didn't have the chance to immediately become a country doctor, because I graduated from the university in the autumn of 1903, just before the outbreak of the war with Japan. The beginning of my medical work was as a military field-surgeon at the hospital of the Kiev Red Cross near the city of Chita.[10]
In our hospital, there were two surgical departments: an experienced surgeon from Odessa was in charge of one of them and the chief doctor of the detachment entrusted me the other one, although there were in the detachment two surgeons much older than me. I immediately took up major surgical operations, operated the wounded, and with no special training in surgery I immediately started doing major critical surgeries on bones, joints and on the skull. The results were quite good, there were no accidents. In my work I was helped a lot by a recently published brilliant book by the French surgeon Lejars[11] "Urgent surgery," which I had studied thoroughly before the trip to the Far East. I was not a staff doctor and I never wore a military uniform.

In Chita, I married a nurse, who had worked in the Kiev military hospital before. There she was addressed as holy sister.[12] She won me not so much by her beauty as by her exceptional kindness and gentle nature. There, two doctors asked for her hand, but she had made the vow of celibacy. By marrying me she broke her vow. So, the night before our holy Matrimony in the church built by the Decembrists she prayed before the icon of the Saviour. Suddenly it seemed to her that Christ turned away His face and His image disappeared from the icon case. It seems it was a reminder of her vow, and the Lord heavily punished her for breaking it with unbearable, pathological jealousy.
We left Chita before the end of the war, and I went to work as a doctor in the Ardatov district in the province of Simbirsk.[13] There I had to manage the hospital. In difficult and misera-

ble conditions I immediately began to operate in all the departments of surgery and ophthalmology.[14] But after a few months I had to give up working in Ardatov because of intolerable obstacles.

It should be noted that from the start in the Ardatov hospital I faced great difficulties and the dangers of the use of general anesthesia with poor assistants, and already there I had the idea that it is necessary if possible to avoid narcosis and substitute it in as wide as possible a range of cases with *local* anesthesia. I decided to go to work in a small hospital, and found one in the village of Verkhniy Lyubazh in Fatezh district in Kursk province. However, there it was not easier, because it was a small local hospital with only ten beds. I began to operate extensively and soon acquired such fame that patients came to me from all quarters, and from other districts of Kursk province and the neighbouring Oryol province as well.

I remember a curious event. A young beggar who had been blind since childhood recovered his sight after surgery. Two months later he collected a lot of blind people from the whole district. In a long chain they led each other by sticks. In the hope of being cured they all came to me.

At this time the first edition of the book by professor Braun[15] "Local anesthesia: its scientific basis and practical use" came out. I eagerly read it and from it I first learned of local anesthesia.[16] A few methods of local anesthesia had very recently been published. I remembered, among other things, that Braun considered it unlikely that it is possible to accomplish local anesthesia of the sciatic nerve. This aroused in me a lively interest in local anesthesia and I set for myself the task to take up the development of new methods for it.

In Lyubazh I came across some very rare and interesting surgical cases, and I wrote there my first two articles about them: "Elephantiasis of the face, plexiform neuroma" and another: "Retrograde strangulation in case of rupture of an intestinal loop."

Excessive fame made my position in Lyubazh unbearable. I had to receive out-patients who came in multitudes. And operate at the hospital from nine o'clock in the morning until the evening. And drive around the rather large locality. And at night investigate under the microscope what had been cut out during the operation. And make drawings of the microscopic preparations for my articles. So, soon even my youthful strength was not sufficient for the tremendous work.

Also my first tracheotomy[17] deserves to be mentioned. It was done in very exceptional circumstances. I came to examine a country school in a village near Lyubazh. Classes had already ended. Suddenly a young woman came running to the school. She was carrying a child that was completely suffocated. He had choked on a small piece of sugar, which had stuck in his throat. I only had a penknife, a bit of cotton wool and a little mercuric chloride solution with me. Nevertheless, I decided to do a tracheotomy and asked the teacher to help me. But she closed her eyes and ran away. The old cleaning lady turned out a bit braver, but she also left me on my own when I started the operation. I put the swaddled baby in my lap and quickly made him a tracheotomy. It couldn't have been done better, it hardly leaked. Instead of a tracheotomy tube I inserted into the trachea a goose quill the old lady had prepared. Unfortunately, the operation did not help, because the piece of sugar had got stuck lower, apparently in the bronchi. The district council transferred me to the Fatezh district hospital, but also there I was not able to work for long. The Fatezh district was a pocket of the rarest of bison[18] and black-hundredists[19]. And the most extreme of them was Batezatul, the chairman of the district council, who became famous long before the war for his bill to force Chinese farmers to emigrate to Russia and send them to landowners as bondservants.

Batezatul considered me a revolutionary for the fact that I had not set out immediately to treat a district police officer when he was ill. I would have had to abandon all my work. So by a resolution of the council I was dismissed from service. This, however, did not end well. On the market day one of the blind men I had cured climbed on a barrel and pronounced a rousing speech about my dismissal. And under his leadership a crowd of people went to smash up the district council, the building of which was on the market square. Only one member of the council was there. From fear he hid under the table. Of course, I quickly had to leave Fatezh. That was in 1909.

In 1907 in Lyubazh my first child was born - Misha. And in the next year, in 1908, my daughter Elena. I had to perform the duties of a midwife myself. From Fatezh I left for Moscow and there for a little less than a year I was an extern at the surgical clinic of professor Dyakonov. According to the rules of this clinic, all doctors-externs had to write a doctoral thesis, and I was proposed the theme "Tuberculosis of the knee joint." After two or three weeks I was invited by professor Dyakonov and he asked how my work on the thesis was going. I replied that I had already read the books, but that I had no interest in the subject. The wise professor listened to my answer with undivided attention, and when he found out that I had my own theme he began to ask about it with lively interest. It turned out that he knew nothing about local anesthesia, and I had to tell him about the book of Braun. To my delight, he asked me to continue working on local anesthesia, and to abandon the proposed theme.[20]

Since my subject demanded anatomical investigations and experiments with injections of coloured gelatin on corpses, I had to go to the institute of topographic anatomy and operative surgery, whose director was professor Rein,[21] chairman of the Moscow surgical society. But it turned out that he had not heard or read anything about local anesthesia.

Soon I was able to find an easy and reliable way to inject near the sciatic nerve at its very exit out of the pelvic cavity, something Heinrich Braun believed to be a hardly solvable problem. I also found a way to inject near the median nerve to achieve regional anesthesia throughout the hand. About these discoveries I gave a lecture at the Moscow surgical society,[22] and it aroused great interest.

But I had nothing I to live from in Moscow with a wife and two young children, so I left to work in a twenty-five bed hospital in Romanovka village in Balashov district in Saratov province.[23] There I organized a large surgical practice. I published a report on it in book form based on the model of the clinic reports of professor Dyakonov. I continued my work on local anesthesia in Moscow during the annual month-long vacations in the institute of professor Rein and professor Karuzin[24] at the subfaculty of descriptive anatomy. I was working from morning to evening there. I examined three hundred skulls and found a very important means to inject near the second branch of the trigeminal nerve at the very exit of the foramen rotundum.[25] By the end of this work I already was no longer in Romanovka, but occupied the position of chief physician and surgeon of a fifty beds district hospital in Pereslavl.[26]

Shortly before we left Romanovka my son Alyosha was born, whilst I had a big adventure. The time of labour drew near, but I took a chance and went to a sanitary board meeting in Balashov, hoping to return soon. I didn't wait for the end of the board meeting and I hurried to the station. There I saw the train. It had already whistled for the second time. I boarded the train without having had time to buy a ticket. Soon I saw there were many Tatars on it, which did not happen in a train to Romanovka. It turned out that I was not in the right train, but in the train to Kharkov, so I had to go back to Balashov from the nearest station. But God stood by, because in Romanovka I found my son already born. A female doctor had received him. She had come back from the sanitary board before me and stopped there on the way to her medical locality. In 1916, while living in Pereslavl, I defended my doctoral thesis on local anesthesia in Moscow. The opponents were professor Martynov,[27] an assistant professor of topographic anatomy and operative surgery whose name I do not remember, and professor Karuzin.

Of interest was the response of professor Martynov. He said: "We are used to doctoral theses generally being written on a prescribed topic, with the purpose of obtaining high functions at work and their scientific value is smallish. But when I read your book, I got the impression of a bird who cannot restrain himself from singing. I highly appreciated the book." And professor Karuzin was very agitated, he ran up to me, shook my hand and painstakingly apologized that he had not been interested in my work in the attic where skulls are preserved. He had no idea that such a brilliant work was being created there.

From the university of Warsaw I received the large Chojnacki prize of nine hundred gold rubles for my thesis. They were intended "for the best works that will lay a new path in medicine." However, I happened not to receive this money, because my book was published in a small edition, only 750 copies, and it was quickly sold out in bookstores where I imprudently had sent them all, and I could not present the university of Warsaw with the required number of copies.

For a country doctor which I was for thirteen years, sundays and holidays are the busiest and the most burdened by an enormous amount of work. So neither in Lyubazh, nor in Romanovka, nor in Pereslavl-Zalessky did I have an opportunity to go to church services and for many years I did not fast. However, in the last years of my life in Pereslavl, I did find the opportunity to visit the cathedral sometimes, although with difficulty. I had my own permanent place there, and this caused great joy among the faithful of Pereslavl.

In my life there was another great development, which the Lord initiated in Pereslavl.

From the beginning of my surgical activity in Chita, Lyubazh and Romanovka I clearly realized the significance of purulent surgery and how little knowledge about it I took with me from the university. I set myself the task to make a profound independent study of the diagnosis and treatment of purulent diseases. At the end of my stay in Pereslavl it came to my mind to document my experience in a separate book: "Essays on purulent surgery." I made a plan for the book and wrote an introduction to it. And then, to my surprise, a very strange persistent thought appeared: "When this book is written, the name of a bishop will be on it."

I had never dreamed of being a clergyman, let alone a bishop, but the omniscient God fully knows our unknown life paths already when we are in our mother's womb. As you will see further on, already in a few years my persistent thought had become a full reality: "When this book is written, the name of a bishop will be on it."

In Pereslavl-Zalessky we lived for 6½ years. There my youngest son Valentin was born.

In the city and the factory hospital, I developed a very extensive surgical practice. I was one of the pioneers in the then new major operations on the biliary tract, stomach, spleen, and even the brain. In addition, in 1915-1916 I headed a small hospital for the wounded.

In early 1917, my wife's elder sister came to us. She had just buried her young daughter in the Crimea. Her daughter had died of galloping consumption. To our great misfortune, she had brought the quilt with her, under which her sick daughter had lain. I told my wife Anna that with the blanket she had brought death to us. And so it happened: Anna's sister lived with us only a couple of weeks, and soon after her departure, I discovered that Anna had obvious signs of pulmonary tuberculosis.

This coincided with the time when through an advertisement in the newspaper with very big competition, I was invited to Tashkent for the post of chief physician and surgeon of a large urban hospital. Our girl-servant who had recently given birth to a child was going with us. Halfway from Pereslavl to Moscow we had to stay for a week at the guesthouse of the Trinity Lavra of Saint Sergius due to Anna having a high fever. The train trip to Moscow and the road further on to Tashkent with small children were extremely difficult because rail traffic was already heavily disturbed.

In Tashkent we had the excellent hospital head physician's flat with five rooms. But I often had to scrub the floors myself because of the disarray of life which is inevitable during a revolution.[28] In 1919 an internecine war went on in the city between the Tashkent fortress garrison and a regiment of Turkmen soldiers under the leadership of a military commissar[29] who had betrayed the revolution. Cannon shells were flying in great numbers from both sides across the whole city and over the hospital, and under them I had to walk to the hospital.

The rebellion of the Turkmen regiment was suppressed. Now the reprisal began against the participants of the counter-revolution. In the process, both I and the hospital household manager had to endure terrible hours. We were arrested by a certain Andrey, a hospital morgue attendant, who nourished hatred against me because he had been punished by the head of the city after a complaint of mine. The hospital household manager and I were taken to the railway workshops where the trial of the Turkmen regiment took place. As we were approaching the railway bridge, workers who were standing on the rails shouted something to Andrey. As I learned later, they advised Andrey not to bother with us and shoot us under the bridge.

A huge room was filled with soldiers of the insurgent regiment, and each in turn was called into a separate room. There they put a cross next to the name of almost everyone on the list. Andrey participated in the tribunal with another hospital employee who managed to warn the other participants of the jury that the household manager and I were arrested by Andrey out of personal malice. They did not put crosses next to our names and we were quickly released. When we were escorted back to the hospital we met workers on the road. They were extremely surprised that we had been released from the workshops.[30]

Later we learned that on the same day in the evening a horrific human carnage had been arranged in the huge barracks of the workshops. The Turkmen regiment and many townspeople were killed.

And my poor sick Anna knew that I was arrested, knew where they had taken me, and lived through terrible hours until my return. This severe emotional shock had an extremely harmful effect on her health, and her disease started progressing rapidly. The last days of her life came. She was burning with fever, completely lost her sleep and suffered greatly. The last twelve nights I sat at her deathbed, whilst working at the hospital during the day. It was the last dreadful night. Anna was dying. In order to alleviate her suffering, I injected her with a syringe of morphine, and she visibly relaxed. Twenty minutes later I heard: "Inject more." Half an hour later this repeated again, and within two or three hours I had injected her with an amount of syringes of morphine far exceeding the permissible dose. But I did not see the effect of morphine poisoning. Suddenly Anna quickly rose and sat up. She said quite loudly: "Call the children." The children came, and she made the sign of the cross over them all, but she did not kiss them, probably for fear of infecting them. Having said farewell to the children she lay down. She lay quietly with her eyes closed, and her breathing was becoming less and less... And she breathed her last breath.

The coffin had been prepared in advance. In the morning my operation assistants came. They washed and dressed the dead body, and laid it in the coffin. Anna died when she was 38 years old, at the end of October 1919, and I was left with four children, of which the oldest was twelve and the youngest six years old.

For two nights I read psalms over the coffin, standing at the feet of the deceased in total solitude. The second night at three I was reading psalm 112. It is sung at the beginning of the meeting of the bishop in the church: "From the rising of the sun unto the going down of the same,"[31] and the last words of the psalm amazed and astonished me, because I perceived them with absolute certainty as words God Himself addressed to me: "He maketh the barren woman to keep house, and to be a joyful mother of children."[32]

The Lord God knew what a heavy and thorny path awaited me, and immediately after the death of the mother of my children He Himself was concerned with them and alleviated my plight. Somehow, without the slightest doubt, I took the astonishing words of the psalm as an indication of God about my operation sister Sofia Sergeyevna Beletskaya, of whom I knew only that she had recently buried her husband and had no children.[33] My acquaintance with her was entirely limited to practical conversations related to the operation at hand. And yet, the words "He maketh the barren woman to keep house, and to be a joyful mother of children" I took without doubting as an indication of God to entrust to her the care of my children and their education.

I could hardly wait for seven in the morning and went to Sofia Sergeyevna, who lived in the surgical department. I knocked on the door. She opened and stepped back because to see her stern supervisor at that hour surprised her. She listened with deep emotion about what happened during the night by my wife's coffin.

I only asked her if she believed in God, and if she wanted to fulfill God's command to replace the deceased mother of my children. Sofia Sergeyevna gladly accepted.

She said that it had been very painful for her to watch from afar how my wife was tormented, and very much wanted to help us, but she did not dare to offer us her help. She had loved my younger children from afar, but she was concerned she would not be able to cope with Misha, my eldest son, because he treated the younger ones badly. It so happened. She loved the three younger children very much. Especially the youngest, Valentin, would not get down from her knees. And Misha she had to re-educate.

My chief physician's apartment consisted of five rooms. The rooms were so well arranged that Sofia Sergeyevna could get a separate room, completely isolated from the ones I took up. She lived with my family, but she was only the second mother to the children, for the almighty God knows that my attitude to her was completely pure. With this I end, and next I will tell you about the great goodness that my children received from God through Sofia Sergeyevna.

Chapter 3. Priesthood

I soon found out that there was a parish brotherhood in Tashkent, and I went to one of its meetings.[34] On the subject of one of the issues that was discussed I made a rather long speech which made a big impression. This impression turned into joy when they found out I was the chief physician of the city hospital.

The eminent archpriest Mikhail Andreyev, rector at the church near the station arranged the parish meetings in the evening on Sundays. There he himself, or someone from the number of those present who wished to do so, could come forward with a talk on a topic of the Holy Scripture. And afterwards all sang spiritual songs. I often attended these meetings, and frequently led serious discussions. Of course, I did not know that they would be just the beginning of my great preaching efforts in the future.

It is well-known that when the bad memory of the "Living" church[35] cropped up everywhere at eparchial meetings clergy and laity discussed the functioning of bishops and some of them were dismissed from the cathedra. Just like that, the "trial" of the bishop of Tashkent and Turkestan took place in Tashkent in the big singing room, very close to the cathedral. I also attended as a guest and on some very important matter I made a long, impassioned speech.

There were no severely critical statements at the meeting and the activities of his eminence Innokenty[36] received a positive evaluation. When the meeting had ended those who had been present dispersed. At the door I unexpectedly bumped into vladyko Innokenty. He took me by the arm and led me to the platform surrounding the cathedral. We walked twice around the cathedral. The bishop said that my speech had made a big impression, and suddenly he stopped and said to me: "Doctor, you should be a priest!"

As I said before, I had never had a thought about the priesthood, but the words of his eminence Innokenty I accepted as God's call through the mouth of the bishop and without a mo-

ment's reflection I said, "Very well, vladyko! I will be a priest, if it pleases God!"
However, later I was talking with vladyko about the fact that my operation nurse Beletskaya lived in my house. I explicitly took her into my house as "a joyful mother of children," but a priest cannot live in the same house with another woman. But vladyko did not attach importance to this objection. He said he did not doubt my loyalty to the seventh commandment.

The next Sunday when the hours were read I already appeared in a borrowed cassock. Accompanied by two deacons I walked to the bishop who was standing on the cathedra. He ordained me as a reader, singer and subdeacon, and during the Liturgy to the rank of deacon.

Of course, this extraordinary event of consecration to the diaconate of someone who had already received the high degree of professor was a huge sensation in Tashkent,[37] and a large group of medical students led by a professor came to me. Of course they could not understand and appreciate my action, for they were far from religion. What would they understand if I told them that when seeing blasphemous carnivals and mockery of our Lord Jesus Christ my heart cried out loud: "I cannot keep mum!" And I felt it was my duty to defend by preaching our violated Saviour and to praise His immeasurable compassion for the human race.

One week after my ordination into the diaconate, at the feast of the Presentation of the Lord in 1921, bishop Innokenty ordained me as a priest.

I forgot to say earlier that in Tashkent I was one of the initiators of founding the university. Most of the cathedrae were filled with a selection from the number of Tashkent doctors of medicine. I was for some reason selected for the cathedra of topographical anatomy and operative surgery,[38] I was the only one nominates in Moscow.

I had to combine my priestly service with reading lectures at the medical faculty. A great number of students from other courses came to listen to them. I read lectures in a cassock with a cross on my chest: at that time what is impossible now was still possible. I also remained chief surgeon of the Tashkent city hospital, because I served in the cathedral only on Sundays.

His eminence Innokenty rarely preached. He appointed me as fourth priest of the cathedral and charged me with all preaching work. Giving me the task, he said to me with the words of the apostle Paul: "Your job is 'not to baptize, but to preach'."[39,40] He had a deep understanding of what he said, and his word was almost prophetic, and now, at the thirty-eigth year of my priesthood and the thirty-sixth year of my archiepiscopacy, I quite clearly understand that my calling from God was exactly preaching and confessing the name of Christ. During the long time of my priesthood I've done hardly any baptisms, marriages and funerals, I've not even once done the full rite of baptism. Besides preaching after the church services which his eminence Innokenty and I performed, every Sunday after vespers in the cathedral I gave long talks on important and difficult theological issues which attracted a lot of listeners. A whole series of these talks was dedicated to a critique of materialism. I did not have a theological education, but with God's help it was easy to overcome the difficulties of such discussions.

In addition, for two years it often fell on me to debate with archpriest Lomakin, a former missionary of the Kursk eparchy who had renounced God and headed the anti-religious propaganda in Central Asia. The debates were public and there was a multitude of listeners.

As a rule, these debates ended with the derision of the apostate from faith. The religious would hound him with the question: "Tell us when you lied: when you were a priest or are you lying now?" The miserable blasphemer of God became afraid of me and asked the organizers of the debates to save him from "that philosopher."

One day, without him knowing about it, the railroad men invited me to their club to take part in a debate about religion. Anticipating the beginning of the dispute I sat on the stage with the curtain down and suddenly I saw my customary opponent walk up the stairs towards the stage. When he saw me he became extremely uneasy and muttered: "Again this doctor." He bowed and walked down. He was the first to speak at the debate, but, as always, my speech completely smashed all his arguments and the workers gave me a loud applause.

For the unfortunate blasphemer of the Holy Spirit the word of the psalmist David came terribly true: "Evil shall slay the wicked."[41] He developed cancer of the rectum and under operation it was found that the tumor had grown into the bladder. In the pelvis soon formed a deep, extremely evil-smelling cavity filled with pus, faeces and urine and infested with a multitude of worms. The enemy of God became extremely hostile because of his sufferings, and even the communist party nurses assigned to care for him could not bear his anger and curses and refused to nurse him.

This time was difficult for me because I had to combine the service and preaching in the cathedral with the management of the sub-faculty of topographical anatomy and operative surgery and reading lectures. Still I also urgently had to study theology. And with this the Lord helped me through one of the listeners of my talks and debates. This was a religious bookseller who brought me so many theological books that soon a decent library came into being in my house.

But this is not yet all: I continued working as the chief physician of the hospital, extensively operated every day and even at night in the hospital, and I could not refrain from processing my observations scientifically. To do this, I often had to do research on corpses in the hospital morgue where carts loaded with piles of corpses were brought in daily. They were the bodies of refugees from the Volga region, where severe famine and epidemics of infectious diseases were raging. I had to start my work on these corpses by cleaning them from lice and night soil with my own hands. Many of these studies on corpses were the basis of my book, "Essays on purulent surgery",[42] that ran into three editions with a circulation of sixty thousand copies. I received the Stalin prize of the first degree for it.

However, working on corpses covered with lice cost me dearly. I contracted relapsing fever in a very severe form, but by the grace of God the disease was limited to one severe attack and a second slight attack.

In the spring of 1923, just before the church schism and the emergence of the Living church, bishop Innokenty convened a congress of clergy from the Tashkent and Turkestan eparchy, which was to elect two candidates to be raised to the rank of bishop. The choice fell on archimandrite Bessarion and me. Soon there was a revolt against patriarch Tikhon of Moscow by Petrograd priests, headed by archpriest Alexander Vvedensky. Throughout Russia, there was a division of the clergy between on the one hand the steadfast and strong in spirit, faithful to the orthodox church and patriarch Tikhon, and on the other hand the faint-hearted, unfaithful, or those who did not understand the stormy church events, who became a member of the Living church led by Vvedensky and a few of his accomplices, whose names I do not remember anymore.

The schism extended to our eparchy in Tashkent. Archbishop Innokenty rarely preached himself. But he made a bold, strong sermon about the fact that there was a rebellion in the church and that it was necessary to remain faithful to the Orthodox church and patriarch Tikhon and not to enter into any relations with the Living church bishop, whose arrival was expected.

Unexpectedly for everybody, two prominent archpriests in whom we were fully confident switched over to the schism, they were joined by others, and not many faithful were left.

His eminence Innokenty hastened to perform the elevation of archimandrite Bessarion. Together with bishop Sergius[43] who had recently been transferred to Tashkent after his exile to Ashgabat, he performed the full rite of nominating[44] Bessarion[45] as a bishop. But the next day, the nominated bishop was arrested and deported from Tashkent. He later joined the Gregorian schism and received the rank of metropolitan.

His eminence Innokenty was very frightened. In the night he secretly left for Moscow, hoping to get to Valaam monastery. But this, of course, he did not manage, and only after a long time was he able to make his way to his village Pustynka.

The bishop had left. In the church there was a rebellion. Then archpriest Mikhail Andreyev and I united all remaining faithful priests and church elders, and staged a congress of the remaining faithful. We had warned the GPU[46] about it, we had asked permission and had asked if they would send observers. Archpriest Andreyev and I took the management of eparchial affairs on ourselves and convened in Tashkent an eparchial meeting of priests and members of the church council who rejected the Living church. We asked the GPU to send their representatives to these meetings, but they never came. It would seem that everything was done faultlessly, but mainly for this I was condemned to my first exile.

At this time a very prominent bishop came to Tashkent, bishop Andrey.[47] Upon learning of our state of affairs, he appointed me as rector of the cathedral and declared me archpriest.

Soon after this another exiled bishop was transferred from Ashgabat to Tashkent: Andrey Ufimsky.[48,49] Shortly before his arrest and exile to Central Asia he was in Moscow and patriarch Tikhon, who was under house arrest, gave him the right to select candidates for elevation to the rank of bishop and to secretly ordain them.

Arriving in Tashkent, his eminence Andrey endorsed my election as a candidate for ordination as bishop by the council of the Tashkent clergy and secretly tonsured me into monkhood[50] in my bedroom. He told me that he had wanted to give me the name Panteleimon, but when he had been at the Liturgy performed by me and had listened to my sermon he found that the name of the apostle-evangelist, physician and iconographer Luke was much more suitable.

His eminence Andrey sent me to the Tajik city of Panjakent at a distance of 90 versts from Samarkand. In Panjakent lived two exiled bishops: Daniel Volkhovsky and Vasily Suzdalsky,[51] bishop Andrey passed them a letter through me asking them to perform my episcopal elevation.

As I wrote above, I was a junior priest of Tashkent cathedral for two years and four months while continuing to work as head physician and surgeon of the city hospital. My departure to Samarkand was supposed to be a secret, so I scheduled four operations on the following day, but in the evening I left by train to Samarkand accompanied by one hieromonk, a deacon and my eldest son Mikhail who was 16 years old.

In the morning we arrived in Samarkand, but to find a two-horse cab to continue our voyage to Panjakent was almost impossible: No one consented to go, because they were all afraid of an attack by Basmachis.[52] Finally one brave man was found who resolved to take us. We rode for a long time. Half way we stopped at a tea house to rest and feed the horses. The last two nights I had not slept for a minute and there, as soon as I lay down on the wooden platform on which Uzbeks drink tea, at that very moment it was as if I fell into an abyss, I slept like a log. I slept only three quarters of an hour, but the sleep strengthened me, and I felt perfectly rested. With God's help, we arrived safely.

The eminent Daniel and Vasily greeted us with love. After reading the letter of bishop Andrey Ukhtomsky they decided to schedule the Liturgy to perform the elevation on the next day and to immediately serve vespers and matins in the little church of hierarch Nicholas of Myra, without ringing and with the doors locked. With the bishops lived the exiled Moscow archpriest Sventsitsky,[53] a well-known religious writer. He was also present at my ordination. During the vespers and the Liturgy my companions and archpriest Sventsitsky were reading and singing.

The eminent Daniel and Vasily were troubled by the circumstance that I was not an archimandrite, and only a hieromonk, and that I did not have a nomination to the rank of bishop. But they did not hesitate for long, because they recalled quite a number of examples of bishop consecrations of hieromonks, and they were reassured. The next morning we all went to the church. They locked the door behind them and did not ring. Immediately they began the service and at the beginning of the Liturgy they performed the elevation.

During the elevation the one who is being ordained leans on the altar and a bishop holds an opened Gospel above his head. This is an important part of the ordination. The prayer is read with which the sacrament of the priesthood is actually accomplished. At this moment I was moved with such a deep emotion that my whole body was shaking. The bishops said afterwards that they had never seen a similar emotion. The eminent Daniel and Vasily and father Sventsitsky returned home from the church a little earlier than I did, and I was met with the episcopal salutation: "Ton despoten kai arkhierea hemon..." I became a bishop on the 18th (31st) May 1923. The next day we returned quite safely to Tashkent.

When patriarch Tikhon was informed about this ordination, he did not hesitate for a moment, approved it and declared it legal.

On Sunday, May 21st, the day of the memory of equal-to-the-apostles Constantine and Helen, I scheduled my first episcopal service. His eminence Innokenty had already left. All the priests of the cathedral had fled like rats from a sinking ship, and my first Sunday vigil and Liturgy I could serve only with one priest, archpriest Mikhail Andreyev.

At this first service of mine his eminence Andrey Ufimsky was present in the altar. He was worried I would not be able to serve without mistakes. But, by the grace of God, there were no mistakes.

The next week passed with no worries, and I celebrated the second Sunday vigil at ease. Back home, I read the rule for the communion of the holy mysteries. At eleven in the evening I heard a knock at the front door. A house search and my first arrest. I bade farewell to the children and Sofia Sergeyevna, and for the first time I went into "a black raven," as they called the cars of the GPU. Thus a beginning was made of eleven years of prison terms and exiles.[54] My four children were in the care of Sofia Sergeyevna. She and the children were kicked out of my chief physician's flat and lodged in a tiny room where they could all be accommodated only because the children made a bunk bed so the room became two-storied. But Sofia Sergeyevna was not expelled from the service, she received twenty rubles per month and with them she fed the children and herself.

I was put in the basement of the GPU. The first interrogation was absolutely ridiculous. I was asked whether I was acquainted with people that were completely unknown to me, whether I had had associations with the Orenburg Cossacks.[55] I knew nothing about them of course.

One night, I was summoned for an interrogation, which lasted for about two hours. It was conducted by a very important Chekist,[56] who later came to hold a very prominent position in the Moscow GPU.[57] He questioned me about my political views and my attitude towards the Soviet regime. Upon hearing that I had always been a democrat, he put the question bluntly: "Who are you, our friend or our enemy?" I answered, "Your friend as well as your enemy. If I was not a Christian, I would probably have been a communist. But you reared up suppression of Christianity, and because of that, of course, I'm not your friend."

For the time being they left me alone and they moved me out of the basement to another, more spacious room. The GPU had hastily adapted a large courtyard with surrounding buildings into a prison. That is where I was kept. On further questioning I was presented with absurd accusations of dealings with the Orenburg Cossacks and other made-up charges. In the years of my priesthood, and of my work as the chief physician of the Tashkent hospital, I never stopped writing my "Essays on purulent surgery," which I wanted to publish in two parts, and I intended to publish them soon. The final essay of the first issue remained to be written: "On purulent inflammation of the middle ear and its complications."

I turned to the head of the prison section in which I was placed with the request to allow me to write this chapter. He was kind enough to grant me the right to write in his office after his work. I soon completed the first issue of my book. On the title page, I wrote: "Bishop Luke. Professor Voyno-Yasenetsky. Essays on purulent surgery."

Thus God's mysterious and incomprehensible prophecy about this book amazingly came true, the prophecy I received in Pereslavl a few years ago: "When this book is written, the name of a bishop will be on it."

I did not succeed to publish the book in two issues, and it was published in one first, far from complete edition, only after my first exile. The name of the bishop was omitted of course.[58]

I was not kept in jail for long and was released for one day for me to go freely to Moscow. All night my former chief hospital physician's apartment was filled with parishioners of the cathedral, who had come to say goodbye to me. At this time, the Tashkent episcopal cathedra was already occupied by Living church metropolitan Nicholas. I called him "a ferocious wild boar who reclines on the High Place.[59]" I forbade people to associate with him. This last will of mine infuriated the Chekists.[60]

In the morning I said farewell to the children and made for the railroad station. I took a seat not in the prisoners' carriage, but in the passengers' carriage. After the first, second and third calls and whistles of the locomotive the train did not move from the spot for twenty minutes. As I found out only after a long time, the train could not move on account of a crowd of people that lay on the tracks. They wanted to keep me in Tashkent, but, of course, this was impossible.

Chapter 4. First exile

In Moscow, I appeared at the central GPU, where after a short meaningless interrogation they declared that for a week I could live freely in Moscow and then I would have to appear again at the GPU. During this week, I twice visited patriarch Tikhon and once I served with him.[61]

At my second appearance at the GPU I was arrested and sent to Butyrskaya prison. After a week's stay in quarantine I was placed in a cell with criminals. In this cell, however, the bandits and thieves treated me pretty well. In the prison hospital, I became acquainted for the first time with Novgorod metropolitan Arseny.[62] In the next cell, also for criminals, there was a priest who had a very big influence on the bandits and thieves. The influence of this priest suddenly ceased when an old sophisticated thief entered the cell. The criminals met him as their leader, with great respect.

Every day we were let out for a walk in the prison yard. Returning from the yard to the second floor, I noticed for the first time that I was breathless.

One day, to my great surprise, I was called for a meeting. I talked with my eldest son Misha through the bars. In the process of searching for work he had experienced many misadventures. In Kiev he had to paint the railroad bridge whilst standing in a cradle hanging above the Dnieper.

At the library of Butyrskaya prison I managed to my delight to get a New Testament in German and I zealously read it. Late in the autumn a large batch of prisoners from Butyrskaya prison were driven on foot across Moscow to Taganka prison. I walked in the first row with not far from me that sophisticated old thief who was the master of the rabble in the cell neighbouring mine in Butyrskaya prison.

In Taganka prison I was not placed with the thieves but in a cell with political prisoners. All prisoners, including myself, received a moderately sized sheepskin from the wife of the writer Maxim Gorky. When I went to the water closet through the long corridor, I saw through a lattice door a shivering half-naked little thief who was sitting against a column in an empty isolation cell, the floor of which was inundated with ankle-deep water. I gave him my short sheepskin coat which I didn't need. This made a huge impression on the old man, the leader of the gang, and every time I passed by the cell for criminals, he greeted me very graciously and called me "father." Later, in other prisons, I repeatedly received evidence that thieves and bandits deeply appreciate a sincere humane attitude towards them.

In Taganka prison I fell ill with a severe flu, probably viral, and I spent about a week in the prison hospital with a temperature of around 40 degrees. From the prison doctor I received a reference in which it was written that I couldn't walk and that I had to be transported on a cart. In the Moscow prisons I had the occasion to sit with archpriest Mikhail Andreyev, who came from Tashkent with me. Together with him I also left Moscow for my first exile early in the winter of 1923.

When the train arrived in the city of Tyumen, it was a quiet moonlight night, and I felt like going to the prison on foot, although the guard offered a cart. The prison was not more than a verst away, but, as ill luck would have it, they hurried us to walk at a fast pace, and I arrived in the prison with severe shortness of breath. My pulse was slight and quick, and on my legs appeared big oedemas up to my knees.

It was the first manifestation of myocarditis. Relapsing fever should be considered the cause of it. I had suffered that in Tashkent, a year after my ordination to the priesthood. In Tyumen prison our stop did not last long, about two weeks. I was lying in bed all the time, without medical help, so I only received a bottle of digitalis after twelve days. In Tyumen prison we met archpriest Hilarion Golubyatnikov for the first time and we travelled on together with him.

The second major stop was in the city of Omsk, but I don't have any memories about it. From Omsk to Novosibirsk we went on a "Stolypin" prisoners' train,[63] in which there were individual cells with barred doors and a narrow corridor with small, highly placed windows. In the cell designated for me and my companions, the two archpriests, were placed, apart from us, a criminal, who had killed eight people, and a prostitute, who went out at night to practice her trade with our guards.

The bandit knew that I had given my coat to the little shivering thief in the Taganka prison, so he was very polite to me. He assured me that nowhere and never anyone from his criminal fraternity would hurt me. However, already in the Novosibirsk prison while I was washing myself in the bath, someone stole a few hundred rubles from me, and later, in that same prison, they stole a whole suitcase full of things.

In this prison they first put us in a separate cell, but soon they transferred us to a large cell for criminals, where the scum met us with such animosity that I had to escape from them: I began banging on the door with the pretext that I needed to go to the water closet and when I got out I told the guard that under no circumstance I would go back in the cell.

From Novosibirsk to Krasnoyarsk we travelled without any particular adventures. In Krasnoyarsk we were put in the large basement of the two-floor building of the GPU. The basement was very dirty and soiled with human excrements, which we had to clean. To do that we were not even given shovels. In the basement next to ours were Cossacks of a rebel brigade. The name of their leader I cannot remember, but I will never forget the sound of the gun salvos that carried to our basement when the Cossacks were executed. We lived for a while in the basement of the GPU, and then we were sent along the winter road to the town of Yeniseysk, three hundred and twenty kilometres north of Krasnoyarsk.

About this journey I remember little, I will only not forget the operation that I had to do on a thirty year old farmer during one of the overnight halts. After heavy osteomyelitis[64] that no one had treated, the whole upper third and the head of the shoulder bone protruded from a gaping wound in the deltoid area. There was nothing to bandage it, and his shirt and his bed were always saturated with pus. I asked to find a metalworker's pincers and without any difficulty I pulled out a huge piece of dead bone (sequestrum.[65])

In Yeniseysk we had a nice apartment in a wealthy man's house and lived in it for about two months. We were joined by another exiled priest, and on Sundays and holidays all of us performed the vigil and Liturgy in our apartment, which included a living room. In Yeniseysk there were a lot of churches, but here, as in Krasnoyarsk, the priests had deviated to the Living church schism, and with them, of course, we could not pray. One deacon had remained faithful to Orthodoxy, and I ordained him as a presbyter.

On one of the holidays I went into the living room to start the Liturgy, and suddenly I saw a strange old monk standing near the opposite door. He was dumbfounded at the sight of me and did not even bow. Having come to himself, he said in response to my question that he was from Krasnoyarsk. He told me that the people there did not want to associate with disloyal priests and decided to send him to the city of Minusinsk, three hundred versts to the south of Krasnoyarsk, to have him ordained as a priest by an orthodox bishop who lived there. His name I do not remember. But monk Christopher did not go to him, because some unknown force drew him to me in Yeniseysk. "Why were you so stunned to see me?" I asked him. "How could I not have been astounded?!" he said. "Ten years ago, I had a dream which I remember as if it were yesterday. I dreamed that I was in a church of God, and an unknown bishop ordained me a hieromonk. Just now, when you came in, I saw that bishop!"

The monk bowed to the ground to me, and during the Liturgy I ordained him a hieromonk.

Ten years back, when he had seen me in his dream, I was still a country surgeon in the city of Pereslavl-Zalessky and never even dreamed about either the priesthood, or episcopacy. And for God at that time I was already a bishop. Such are the inscrutable ways of the Lord.

My visit to Yeniseysk was a very big sensation, which came to a culmination when I extracted congenital cataracts[66] from the eyes of three little blind boys, brothers, and made them see. At the request of doctor Vasily Aleksandrovich Bashurov, who was in charge of the Yeniseysk hospital, I began to operate and in the two months of my life in Yeniseysk I did a lot of very important surgical and gynaecological operations. At the same time, I received a lot of patients in my own home, and there were so many who wanted to be treated that from the first days it was necessary to make appointments with the patients. This agenda, which was started in early March, was soon filled until Pentecost.[67]

Shortly before I arrived in Yeniseysk the convent had been closed. Two novices of this convent told me with what blasphemy and desecration closing this church of God was accompanied.[68] It went so far that a Komsomol[69] member, who had been among those who had ravaged the convent, lifted all her skirts, and sat on the bishop's throne. These two novices I tonsured into monkhood and I gave them the names of my heavenly patrons: the older one I named Lukiya and the younger, Valentina.

Shortly before the feast of Annunciation I was sent to the place of exile appointed to me - the village of Chaya[70] on the river Chunia, a tributary of the Angara. Lukiya and Valentina went ahead of me with our things, and archpriests Hilarion Golubyatnikov and Mikhail Andreyev went with me till the village of Boguchany. We rode on horseback on the frozen Yenisei and Angara until Boguchany, where we were separated. They sent archpriests Golubyatnikov and Andreyev to a village not far from Boguchany, and me hundred and twenty versts away, to the village of Chaya. In Boguchany I operated on a patient who had a festering echinococcus[71] of the liver, and in a few months, when I came back from Chaya, I found him quite healthy.

In Boguchany I was designated a pious farmer in the village of Chaya, where I was advised to move in, but they warned that he had a nasty old mother. In Chaya my nuns had already settled in with the farmer and they were waiting for me. The old mother met me with great joy. For me two rooms were set aside, in one of which we performed divine services with the nuns, and in the other I slept. The angry old mother came to our worship only on the first days, and then she kept to her own half of the house. And not only that, but she tried in every possible way to disturb our services.

The angry old woman increasingly harassed us and began to actually make us leave. It came so far that the nuns and I took our things out of the house and sat on them against the wall. Seeing that we were kicked out of the house, the people were outraged and forced the old woman to take us back into the house.

In Chaya I had to operate, in exceptional circumstances, on an old man who had a cataract. I had a set of eye instruments and a little sterilizer with me. In an empty uninhabited log hut I put the old man on a narrow bench under the window and all alone I did a cataract extraction on him. The surgery was quite successful. I received ten squirrel pelts for it. They were worth a ruble each. I also had the chance to perform a burial service for a farmer with my nuns according to the Easter rite.

In Chaya we spent a couple of months until an order was received to send me back to Yeniseysk. We were given two peasants as escorts and riding horses. The nuns first sat on the horses. Very large gadflies stung the animals so mercilessly, that streams of blood were running down their sides and legs. The horse which nun Lukiya rode lay down more than once and rolled on the ground to get rid of the gadflies. Once, the horse heavily came down on her leg.

Halfway to Boguchany we spent the night in a forest hut, despite the demand of the escorts to go on all night. The only thing that had worked was my threat that they would stand trial for inhuman treatment of me, a professor. Before reaching Boguchany with ten versts to go, we stopped riding on horseback. My escort had to take me off my horse, because I had never before travelled on horseback and I was extremely tired. We rode the rest of the way to Boguchany on a cart. After that we travelled on the Angara river by boat, and at that we had to pass dangerous rapids. In the evening, on the bank of the Yenisei river, opposite the mouth of the Angara, the nuns and I served under the open sky an unforgettable vespers.

On arrival in Yeniseysk I was locked up in a solitary cell. At night I was exposed to such an attack of bugs as could not be imagined. I quickly fell asleep, but soon woke up. I switched on the electric light bulb, and saw that the whole pillow and bed and the cell walls were covered by an almost solid layer of bugs. I lit a candle and began to burn some bugs. They fell on the floor from the walls and the bed. The effect of this burning was striking. An hour of burning later there was not a single bug left in the cell. They evidently somehow said to each other: "Save yourselves, brothers! They are burning us here!" The following days I did not see any bugs anymore, they all went to other cells. They kept me briefly in the Yeniseysk jail and then sent me further on down the Yenisei with a caravan from Krasnoyarsk consisting of a small ship and several barges in tow. I was placed in one of these barges with social revolutionaries who were sent to the Turukhansk province. The nuns Lukiya and Valentine wanted to see me off, but they were not allowed to.

The journey on the wide Yenisei that flows through the boundless taiga was boring and monotonous. Halfway to Turukhansk there was a short stop in a fairly large village, the name of which I do not remember. On the shore I was met by a large group of exiles who had come out to meet every steamer in the hope of seeing me, because there they had somehow heard about my exile to Turukhansk. Out of this group, a presbyter from the Leningrad Baptist community, Shilov, came up to me to introduce himself. He had waited for me with particular impatience. Later he came to me in Turukhansk for long conversations.

At a little distance stood another group of people who had been waiting for me too. These were Tungus people, all trachoma[72] patients. One of them, a man half-blind from folded eyelids, I invited to visit me in the hospital in Turukhansk for an operation. He soon followed my advice, and I did a mucous membrane transplantation from his lips to his eyelids.

In Turukhansk when I left the barge, a crowd of people was waiting for me. They suddenly fell to their knees, asking for blessings. I was immediately placed in the apartment of a hospital doctor and they proposed that I direct medical work.[73] Shortly before, the hospital doctor, late at recognizing cancer of the lower lip, had gone to Krasnoyarsk where he underwent surgery. Belated, as it turned out later. In the hospital there remained a paramedic, and together with me a nurse had come from Krasnoyarsk, a young girl who had just graduated from medical school and who was very excited at the prospect of working with a professor. With these two assistants, I did such big operations as resection of the upper jaw, large laparotomies, gynaecological surgery and a lot of eye operations.

The ice on the Yenisei started drifting already when, to my surprise, Leningrad Baptist presbyter Shilov came to me. He had travelled for seven hundred versts by boat. Shilov had undertaken this dangerous, heavy journey just to talk to me. Before him there arrived a puny little Jew to Turukhansk. He had come from America to Moscow under the guise of a communist, but something had stirred suspicion and he had been imprisoned in the vacated Solovetsky monastery.

This little Jew was once present during a conversation of mine with Shilov, and at his request I allowed him to attend our talks, which lasted for three days for a few hours a day. Shilov asked me to examine a number of texts from Scripture, and of course I explained them in the spirit of orthodoxy. But in a strange way it turned out, as we shall see later, that Shilov convinced me of the rightness of baptism. Our conversations ended. Shilov managed to return to Krasnoyarsk on some delayed steamer.

The Turukhansk monastery was closed. However, an old priest performed all church services there.[74] He was subject to the Krasnoyarsk Living church bishop, and I had to turn him and the whole Turukhansk congregation back on to the path of fidelity to ancient orthodoxy. This was achieved by a sermon about the great sin of the schism: the priest repented before the people, and I could come to church services and almost always preached at them. The Turukhansk peasants were deeply grateful to me and brought me to the monastery and home on a carpeted sledge. At the hospital, of course, I did not refuse anyone the blessing,[75] which Tungus very much appreciated and always requested. For this and for the church sermons I had to pay dearly.

I was warned that the chairman of the provincial council of Turukhansk was a great enemy and hater of religion. This, however, did not prevent him to cry out to God for salvation, when he got into a violent storm on the Yenisei River in a small boat. At the request of this chairman the GPU commissioner called me and announced that I was strictly forbidden to bless the sick in the hospital, to preach in the monastery and to go there on a carpeted sledge. I replied that because it is a bishop's duty I cannot refuse people the blessing, and proposed that he should hang an announcement on the hospital doors that it is forbidden for patients to ask me a blessing. This, of course, he could not do. About the trips to the church, I also proposed him to forbid farmers to give me a carpeted sleigh. He also did not do this.

However, he did not have patience with my resoluteness for long. The building of the GPU was right next to the hospital. I was called there and at the front door I saw a two-horse sleigh with a policeman. The GPU commissioner greeted me with great anger and declared that for non-compliance with the requirements of the executive committee, I had to leave Turukhansk immediately[76] and for packing I was given half

an hour. I calmly asked only: where exactly am I sent to? And I got the irritated reply: "To the Arctic Ocean."
I calmly went to the hospital and the policeman came after me. He whispered in my ear: "Please, please, professor, get ready as soon as possible: we only need to leave from here as soon as possible and get to the nearest village, and then we'll travel at ease." Soon we reached the village of Selivanikha, not far from Turukhansk, which received its name from the name of the leader of the skoptsi sect, Selivanov, who had spent his exile there.
Soon my companions on this exile gathered. They were social revolutionaries. They showed great interest in me and conversed with me for long. They provided me with money and a fur blanket, which was very useful to me.[77] After an overnight stay in the assembly hut we rode on.
The journey on the frozen Yenisei in the bitter frost was very hard for me. However, especially in this difficult time, I felt very clearly, almost actually, that the Lord God Jesus Christ was close to me, that he supported and strengthened me.
We spent the nights at coastal stations. Then we reached the northern polar circle, after which there was a village the name of which I do not remember. Stalin had lived there in exile.[78]
When we entered the log hut, the owner gave me her hand. I asked: "Are you not Orthodox? Do you really not know you should ask a bishop for a blessing and not give a hand?" This, as it turned out later, made a very big impression on the policeman who escorted me. Also before, on the way from Selivanikha to the next station he had told me: "I feel myself in the position of Malyuta Skuratov carrying metropolitan Philip to Otroch monastery."[79]
Our next night was at a station with two houses, in which lived a stern old man called Afinogen with his four sons in the conditions of a medieval feudal baron. He had appropriated for himself the exclusive right to fish in the Yenisei River on a stretch of forty versts, and no one dared to dispute this right. The youngest of the old man's sons was a marvelous example of pathological laziness. He refused all work and for days on end he would be lying in bed. Many times he had been fiercely beaten half to death, but nothing worked. The old man Afinogen considered himself an exemplary Christian and loved to

read the Holy Scriptures. I talked with him late into the night, explaining him what he misunderstood.

The road further on was even more difficult. One of the next stations had recently burned down. We could not stay there for the night and barely got reindeer. The ones we had were weakened from lack of food. We had to ride on them to the next station. After riding non-stop for at least seventy versts I was very weak and so numb that I had to be carried into the log hut and warmed up for a long time. Continuing on the road to the station of Plakhino at a distance of two hundred and thirty versts from the polar circle there were no adventures. My Komsomol escort had been commissioned to choose a place of exile for me himself, as he expressed it, and he had decided to leave me in Plakhino.

This was a small station altogether. It consisted of three cottages and two more, which I took to be large piles of manure and straw, but which in reality were the dwellings of two small families. We went into the main house and before long the very few residents of Plakhino also came in in a single file. All bowed low, and the chairman of the station told me, "Your eminence! Please do not worry about anything, we will arrange everything for you." He introduced me one after the other to the men and women, and said: "Please, do not worry about anything. We have already discussed everything. Every man is obliged to provide you with half a sazhen[80] of firewood per month. This woman here will cook for you, and this one will iron. Please do not worry about anything." Everyone asked for a blessing and they showed me the living quarters that were made ready for me in another log hut, a hut divided into two parts. In one part lived a young farmer and his wife. They were moved to the other part of the house, making it more crowded for those already living there. My Komsomol escort carefully watched the whole scene of my acquaintance with the inhabitants of the station. Now he had to leave to spend the night at the trading post, a few kilometers from Plakhino. It was obvious that he was worried about the prospect of parting with me. But I helped him out of his difficulty by blessing him and giving him a kiss. This, as we shall see later in this narrative, made a strong impression on him.

I was left alone in my room. It was a fairly spacious part of the house with two windows. In each window was placed a flat ice block on the outside instead of a second frame. The cracks in the windows weren't sealed with anything. In places in the outer corner daylight was visible through a large crack. On the floor in the corner was a heap of snow. A second heap like that lay inside the hut ont the threshold of the front door, never melting. To sleep at night and rest during the day the peasants had constructed a wide plank bed and covered it with reindeer skins. I had a pillow with me. Near the plank bed stood an iron stove, which I filled with wood and lighted at night. Lying on the plank bed I covered myself with my raccoon coat and the fur blanket that was given to me in Selivanikha. At night I was scared by the flares of the flames in the iron stove, and in the morning when I got up, I was seized by the frost in the log hut, which formed a thick layer of ice that covered the water in a bucket.

On the first day I began to seal the cracks in the windows with flour paste and thick brown wrapping paper from shopping at the trading post. I also tried to close the crack in the corner of the hut with it. All day and all night, I stoked the iron stove. When sitting at a table dressed warmly, then above the waist it was warm, and below it was cold. Once I had to wash myself in such cold. They brought me a washbowl and two buckets of water: one cold, with chunks of ice, and the other hot, and I don't understand how I contrived to wash myself in such conditions. Sometimes at night something like a most powerful crash of thunder woke me, but it was not thunder, but the ice cracking across the whole wide Yenisei.

Not for long did I get food from the woman who had been charged to cook for me: she had had a fight with her lover and refused to cook food for me. For the first time in my life I had to try to prepare my own food myself, and I had no idea about cooking. The farmers brought me fish and other products they bought at the trading post. I already don't remember what curious result I got when trying to fry fish, but I do remember how I cooked kissel.[81] I cooked cranberries and began to pour liquid starch in it. No matter how much of it I poured, it seemed to me the jelly was too thin, so I continued to pour starch until the jelly suddenly turned into a solid mass. Having suffered a fiasco with my cooking, I had to capitulate, and another woman took pity on me and began to cook for me.

I had the New Testament with me from which I never parted on my exiles. Also in Plakhino I offered the peasants to read and explain the Gospel to them. They responded to that as if they were happy with it, but their joy was short-lived. With each new reading the audience became smaller and smaller, and soon my reading and preaching stopped.

I'll tell about one more work of God, which I had to carry out in Plakhino. Now, when writing these memoirs, I am already more than thirty seven years in the clergy, and more than thirty five years an eparchial bishop, but, oddly enough, I have only baptized three children: one who was close to death, with an abbreviated rite and the other two in a quite unusual way.

In my most distant exile, two hundred and twenty versts beyond the polar circle at the station of Plakhino, I had to baptize two small children in a very unusual setting. As I said already, at the station apart from the three huts there were two more dwellings for people, one of which I took for a haystack, and the other for a pile of manure. There, in the latter, I had to baptize. I had nothing: no robes, no book of needs,[82] and in the absence of the latter I composed prayers myself and from towels I made the likeness of a stole. The wretched human dwelling was so low that I could only stand bent over. A wooden tub served as baptismal font, and the whole time of fulfilling the mystery I was hampered by a calf that was turning about next to the font.

And now, as a bishop, I don't have to baptize, because my priests baptize.

In Plakhino it is often freezing very hard, and there are no crows or sparrows, because with such a cold, they could freeze in mid-flight and fall to the ground like a stone. In the two months of my life in Plakhino I only once saw a small bird sitting on a bush. It was like a big wad of pink down. Once

I had to experience a very hard frost when for several days on end a northern wind, called "Sheaver" by the local people, was constantly blowing. It is a quite icy wind that ceases neither by night nor by day. Horses and cows barely stand it. Day and night the poor animals stand motionless, turning their back to the north.

In the attic of my house were hung fishing nets with large wooden floats. When the "Sheaver" was blowing the floats were constantly clattering, and this clatter reminded me of music by Grieg: "Dance of the dead." Of course, during the day and the night, when it was snowing and freezing, I always had to go out of the house to relieve myself. This was extremely strenuous, but when the "Sheaver" was blowing the situation was desperate. In Plakhino I spent a little more than two months,[83] until the beginning of March, and there were no travellers who passed by the station.

It was only at the beginning of March that the Lord suddenly sent me deliverance. At the beginning of Lent a messenger arrived in Plakhino from Turukhansk and brought me a letter in which the GPU commissioner politely asked me to come back to Turukhansk. I did not understand what had happened, why I was called back to Turukhansk, and only after returning there did I find out. It turned out that at the Turukhansk hospital a farmer had died. He had needed urgent surgery which they could not do without me. This had so angered the Turukhansk peasants that they armed themselves with pitchforks, scythes and axes, and decided to organize a pogrom of the GPU and the village council. The Turukhansk authorities were so frightened that they immediately sent a messenger to me in Plakhino.

The way back to Turukhansk was not too difficult, and only at the station of Afinogen did I experience some unpleasantness. Afinogen sent one of his sons to take me to the station, where Stalin had lived. The horse moved all the time at a walking pace, and the driver did not want to urge it on. I could not stand it, ripped the reins out of the hands of the driver and began to whip the horse. The driver jumped out of the sleigh and ran back. I had no choice but to turn the horse and ride back to Afinogen's house at a walking pace. This "true Christian" swore at me, a bishop, extremely rudely, but his anger immediately subsided when he received a five-ruble gold coin from me. He gave me a couple of good horses, and another son as a driver.

At one of the next stations I experienced travelling with dogs: six very strong Siberian husky dogs were harnessed to the sledge. They ran well, but suddenly one of them bit another, this other one bit a third, and all tumbled into a scuffling pile. The driver jumped out and began to thrash the dogs with the wooden pole which served to drive the dogs. Order was restored, and the dogs safely took us to the place of our destination.

The first person I met in Turukhansk was the same Komsomol policeman, who drove me from Turukhansk to Plakhino. He met me with open arms and genuine joy.

Again I started working at the hospital. The GPU commissioner, who had expelled me from Turukhansk with great anger and gnashing of teeth to the north down the Yenisei, because of my disobedience, met me with exquisite politeness and inquired about my health and life in Plakhino.

Once there was a piquant incident. The commissioner came to me in the hospital on some business. During my conversation with him, the door opened and a whole file of Tungus entered the room with folded hands to ask my blessing. I stood up and blessed them all, but the commissioner pretended not to notice this. And of course I continued to ride to the monastery on a carpeted sledge.

This second stay of mine in Turukhansk lasted for eight months,[84] from Annunciation to November.

In the middle of the summer, I do not remember exactly in what form, I had, as I thought, a prediction from God about my imminent return from my exile in Turukhansk. I looked forward to the fulfillment of this promise, but week after week passed, and everything remained as it was. I became depressed. One day I prayed with tears in front of the icon of the Lord Jesus Christ in the altar of the winter church, which was connected with a door to the summer church. In this prayer I was evidently also grumbling against the Lord Jesus because the promise of liberation had remained unfulfilled already for so long. And suddenly I saw Jesus Christ who was depicted on the icon, abruptly turn away His most pure face from me. I was terrified and despaired and did not dare to look at the icon any more. Like a beaten dog I went out of the altar to the summer church where I saw the book "Acts of the Apostles" in the choir. Mechanically I opened it and I read the first thing that caught my eye.

Much to my distress, I did not memorize the text I read, but this text had a downright miraculous effect on me. It revealed my folly and impertinence to grumble at God and at the same time confirmed the promise of liberation which I eagerly anticipated.

I went back to the altar in the winter church and I was glad to see that when I looked at the icon Jesus looked at me again with gracious and clear eyes.

Is this not a miracle?!

CHAPTER 5. BEFORE THE SECOND EXILE

The end of my exile in Turukhansk came near. From the lower reaches of the Yenisei came, one after the other, ships bringing many of my comrades in exile, who had received the same term at the same time as me. Our term was over. And these steamers were to take us to Krasnoyarsk. From day to day ships came alone and in groups. But I was not called to the GPU to get documents.
One evening at the end of August the last boat came and on the next morning it had to leave. I was not called, and I was worried, because I did not know that there was an order to detain me for another year.
In the morning of August 20th I read the matins as usual, but the ship already was giving out steam. The first long-drawn-out whistle of the steamboat... I read the fourth kathisma of the Psalter... The last words of the 31st Psalm hit me like a thunderbolt... I took them with my whole being as the voice of God, addressed to me. He says: "I will instruct thee and teach thee in the way which thou shalt go: I will guide thee with Mine eye. Be ye not as the horse, or as the mule, which have no understanding: whose mouth must be held in with bit and bridle, lest they come near unto thee."[85]
And suddenly there comes a deep peace in my distraught soul... The steamer whistles a third time and slowly casts off. I watch it go with a quiet and joyful smile as it is hidden from my eyes. "Go, go, I don't need you... the Lord has prepared for me a different path, not the path of a dirty barge that you go, but a light, episcopal path!"
After three months, and not a year later, the Lord enjoined to let me go by sending me a small varicose ulcer of the shin with a bright skin inflammation around it. They were obliged to let me go to Krasnoyarsk.
The Yenisei had frozen up in chaotic heaps of huge ice floes. The sled road on it should be established only by the middle of January. Only one other exile - social revolutionary Chudinov – had been detained when the last ships were sailing and he was to go with me. His wife and ten-year old daughter had

come with him in exile, but his wife had suddenly died in Turukhansk.

For some time past, I had steadily noticed Chudinov standing in the church near the door. He had been carefully listening to my preaching. On the Yenisei, people were driven usually only on sledges, but for me the peasants made a closed sleigh. The long-awaited day came... I had to go by the monastery church which stood on the outskirts of Turukhansk. There I had preached a lot, and sometimes even served. At the church I was met by the priest with a cross and a large crowd of people.

The priest told me about an unusual occurrence. At the end of the Liturgy he had put out all the candles in the church together with the churchwarden. But when he went into the church to prepare to see me off, suddenly one candle lit up in a chandelier. It flickered for a minute and went out.

That's how my favorite church saw me off. I dearly loved this church in which lay hidden away the remains of the holy martyr Vasily Mangazeysky.

The arduous journey on the Yenisei River was the light episcopal path about which at the departure of the last steamer, God Himself foretold me with the words of Psalm 31: "I will instruct thee and teach thee in the way which thou shalt go: I will guide thee with Mine eye." I will watch how you will go this way, but you do not break out to the steamer "as the horse, or as the mule, which have no understanding: whose mouth must be held in with bit and bridle."

My journey on the Yenisei River was truly an episcopal way, because at all the stops I was met with bell ringing if there was an affiliated church. Some of them were even operating churches. I served a moleben and preached there.

And in these places they had not seen a bishop since the most distant times.

In a large village, four hundred versts to go before Yeniseysk, they let us know that to go further was dangerous, because on the Yenisei a wide crack had appeared in the ice, and near the banks the water had gone out on top of the ice, creating so-called "shore ice," and there were no roads in the riverside taiga. However, we moved on all the same.

We rode to the wide crack across the river. The crack was more than a meter wide. We saw a horse with sleigh drowning in it. A poor woman tried in vain to pull the horse out. We helped her, and managed to drag the horse and sleigh out. Then we ourselves became thoughtful about what to do. My driver, a dashing curly headed guy, did not hesitate, and after him also the driver of Chudinov. They just said, "Hold on tight!" They stood up straight, yelled wildly at the horses and whipped them. The horses dashed off with all their might and jumped over the unfrozen patch of water, and behind them also our sled flew through the air.

From Turukhansk to Krasnoyarsk we drove for a month and a half. Every day we travelled from one station to the next, on average forty versts. I was dressed in Tungusic fur clothing and I covered my legs with a raccoon coat. Once the driver asked me to hold the reins while he adjusted the harnesses of the horses. I was wearing rabbit mittens, but as soon as I took my hands out from under the coat and took the reins, my hands burned like fire. The frost was that severe.

In some stations my former patients whom I had operated in Turukhansk came to me. I particularly remembered an old Tungus, half-blind from trachoma, on whom I had remedied inward folding eyelids by a transplant of mucous membrane. The result of the operation was so good that he was shooting squirrels as before, hitting them right in the eye. A boy that had been operated on account of an extremely neglected osteomyelitis of the hip walked up to me, healthy. There were other similar encounters.

We safely arrived in Yeniseysk where the clergy had formerly been entirely renovationist, but converted to the path of truth by me before I had left for Turukhansk. Now the clergy had prepared a ceremonial reception. When we finished the thanksgiving moleben we drove on and after three hundred and twenty versts we came to Krasnoyarsk, two days before the feast of Christmas.

In autumn in Krasnoyarsk, a great number of people had come in vain to meet every boat from the lower reaches of the Yenisei in anticipation of my arrival. And now they did not manage to give me a reception.

We headed for bishop Amphilochius. His attendant, monk Meletius, was blind in one eye due to a central cataract of the cornea, and an optical iridectomy[86] had to be done on him. I sent him to the chief doctor of the hospital with a letter in which I asked him permission to do this operation in the eye department. This request was readily granted. When the next day I came to the hospital with Meletius, I unexpectedly saw a crowd of doctors in the eye department who had come to look at my surgery.

After I had quickly finished the iridectomy, I expressed my regrets that I could not show the doctors the operation of removing the lacrimal sac, which would be much more interesting for them. But right then I was told that there was a patient in the hospital, waiting for this operation. They quickly prepared him while I told the doctors, how I would perform this operation. I started with a detailed description of the topographic anatomy of the lacrimal sac, and I described my method of local anesthesia. Then I began the operation, and step by step, I demonstrated them all that I had just told them. The operation took place without any pain and almost bloodless.

The next day Chudinov and I had to appear at the GPU, and in the hallway of the second floor we were waiting to be called in. I was called first, to the third floor. The interrogation was begun politely by a young Chekist, but soon the assistant head of the GPU came in. He interrupted the questioning and ordered another to do it. That one pulled out an interrogation list and started asking me about my obstinate and courageous squabbles with the Turukhansk GPU commissioner. I answered without justifying myself, and then on my side, I accused the commissioner and the chairman of the district executive committee. The Chekist who recorded my answers was confused and evidently embarrassed.

Again the assistant head of the GPU came in. He read the notes of the interrogating Chekist over his shoulder and threw them in a drawer. To my surprise, he suddenly changed his previous harsh tone and pointing out of the window at the renovationist cathedral he said to me: "These here we despise, and such as you we respect a lot." He asked me where I intended to go and this surprised me. "What, can I really go where I want?" "Yes, of course." "Even to Tashkent?" "Of course, also to Tashkent. Only please, leave as soon as possible." "But tomorrow is the great feast of Christmas, and I must definitely be in the church." The head consented to this with difficulty, but he asked me to definitely leave after the Liturgy.

"You will receive a train ticket and you will be taken to the station. Please, please, we'll drive you there." He and the Chekist who had interrogated me, very politely escorted me down to that courtyard that was memorable to me, from which one door led into the large basement soiled with excrements, in which my companions and I had been kept before being sent to Yeniseysk, and another door led to another basement, in which executions were carried out when we were there.

In this courtyard the head put me in a car with exquisite politeness and he ordered the Chekist to accompany me to the apartment where I was staying.

I knew from experience how dangerous it is to believe the words of Chekists, so I anxiously waited to see where the car would turn at the place where the road to the left leads to the prison and the road to the right to the orthodox cathedral. Near the cathedral the Chekist rang at the gates. The landlady came out and he told her that she was not to worry about my registration. He politely took leave and drove off, and I went across the street to the cathedral, where bishop Amphilochius lived.

Already at the beginning of my conversation with him monk Meletius came in. He reported that a gentleman had come running, very much out of breath. He asked permission to see me. I guessed at once it was Chudinov. He had anxiously run after the car which had driven me, and like me he had been agonized waiting whether the car would turn right to the cathedral or left to the jail.

After receiving permission from his eminence Amphilochius, Chudinov ran into the room. He had been worried to the extreme, and, sobbing, he fell to his knees at my feet. When he had received a blessing from me and bishop Amphilochius, he asked both of us to pray for the repose of the soul of his ten year old daughter who had died in Turukhansk.

After the Christmas vespers and Liturgy, which I served with the Krasnoyarsk bishop Amphilochius, I was given a two-horse phaeton[87] of the GPU, and with Chudinov I went to the station. Halfway we were suddenly stopped by a young police officer. He jumped on the footboard and started hugging and kissing me. It was the police officer who had taken me from Turukhansk to the station Plakhino, two hundred and thirty versts north of the polar circle.

At the station a large crowd of people who had come to see me off was already waiting for me.
I returned to Tashkent through the city of Cherkasy in Kiev province. My parents end eldest brother Vladimir lived in Cherkasy. From Krasnoyarsk I reached Cherkasy quite safely. I travelled together with Chudinov but in Omsk I had to send a telegram to Cherkasy. The stop was short, and the telegraph office was located on the top floor, so I did not manage to run back down before the train moved on. I wired Chudinov, and he left my things at the next station where I got them later. But my good companion had travelled to the Archhangelsk province, and I never met him again.
The meeting of my elderly parents with their son - a professor of surgery who had become a bishop - was touching. They kissed the hand of their son lovingly, with tears they listened to the memorial service which I served over the grave of my deceased sister Olga.
From Cherkasy I finally returned to Tashkent. That was in late January 1926. In Tashkent, I stayed in the apartment where Sofia Sergeyevna Beletskaya lived with my children. She had nurtured and raised them, and sent them to school during my exile.
The first who came to me with congratulations were four principal members of the baptist community. They behaved clearly confusedly, and for me the purpose of their visit was not clear. I later learned that they had received a telegram from the baptist presbyter Shilov from Leningrad, in which he instructed them to welcome me as a new brother of the baptists. Of course, I had to disappoint them in this. I let them know through a certain Nalivaiko who had been a zealous parishioner of the cathedral before, but who had then switched over to the baptist congregation.
At this time the cathedral had already been destroyed and an exiled bishop who had converted to renovationism during my exile had served in the church of venerable Sergius of Radonezh several times.
Archpriest Mikhail Andreyev, who had shared with me the hardship of exile to the Yenisei region and further in Boguchany and who had returned shortly before me, demanded that I would consecrate the Sergius church again after the visit of the bishop, who had switched over to renovationism. I re-

fused to fulfill this request, and this was the beginning of a lot of sorrow. Archpriest Andreyev left his subordination to me and began to serve at home for a small group of like-minded people.

He wrote about me on repeated occasions to the patriarchal locum tenens metropolitan Sergius and even went to see him, and he was able to set up the locum tenens against me. In September of the same year I received from him three decrees, quickly following each other, to transfer me from the eparchial cathedra of the city of Tashkent to the city of Rylsk in the Kursk province, then to the city of Yelets as a vicar of the bishop of Orlov and, finally, to Izhevsk as an eparchial bishop.

I wanted to compliantly submit to these transfers, but metropolitan Arseny of Novgorod, who lived in Tashkent in the position of exile and was formerly a great friend to me and my children, emphatically advised me not to go anywhere, and to forward a petition of resignation to retire.

It seemed to me that I should follow the advice of the venerable hierarch, who had been one of the three candidates for the patriarchal throne at the council of 1917. I followed his advice and was dismissed in 1927. This was the beginning of a sinful path and God's punishments for it. Metropolitan Nikander, also a former exile in Tashkent, replaced me as bishop of Tashkent.

I was only occupied with receiving patients at my home, so of course I did not cease to pray in the Sergius church at all the services,[88] standing in the altar with metropolitan Arseny.

In the spring of 1930 it became known that the church of saint Sergius was destined to be destroyed. I could not bear it, and when the appointed time for closing the church approached, and the dreaded day of closing it had been set, I made a firm decision: to serve on this day the last Liturgy and after that, when the enemies of God were to appear, to shut the church doors, take down all the biggest wooden icons and put them in the middle of the church on a pile, pour gasoline over them, and in episcopal robes climb onto them, set fire to the petrol with a match and be burned in the bonfire... I could not tolerate the destruction of the church... To remain alive and to endure the horrors of the desecration and destruction of God's churches was unbearable for me. I thought my self-immolation would intimidate and bring to reason God's enemies, the enemies of religion, and stop the destruction of churches that spilled like a colossal diabolical wave across the face of the Russian land. But it so pleased God that I did not die at the very beginning of my episcopal service, and according to His will the closing of the Sergius church was somehow delayed for a short time. But I was arrested on that very day.

On April 23rd, 1930, I was at the Liturgy in the Sergius church for the last time, and while reading the Gospel I suddenly with full certitude became certain that on that same evening I would be arrested. And so it happened, and the church was destroyed when I was in prison.

In the famous Easter sermon of saint John Chrysostom he says that God not only "accepts works," but also "kisses intentions." For my intention to die a martyr may the Lord forgive me the great number of my sins!

Chapter 6. Exile to Archangelsk

On April 23rd, 1930, I was arrested for the second time.[89] During interrogations, I soon realized that they wanted me to renounce the priesthood. Then I went on hunger strike to protest. Usually they did not pay attention to announcements about going on hunger strike and left prisoners without food in their cell until their condition became dangerous, and only then they were transferred to the prison hospital. But I was already sent to the hospital early in the morning after having declared I would be going on hunger strike. I fasted for seven days. Quickly my heart grew weaker, and in the end I was vomiting blood. This very much troubled the head physician of the GPU, who came to see me every day. On the eighth day of the hunger strike, around noon, I dozed off and in a dream I felt a group of people standing at the side of my bed. When I opened my eyes, I saw a group of Chekists and doctors and the famous physician, professor Slonim. The doctors examined my heart and whispered to the chief Chekist that it was a bad case. There was an order to carry me on the bed to the prison doctor's office, where not even professor Slonim was allowed to stay.
The chief Chekist told me, "Let me introduce myself - you do not know me - I'm deputy head of the Central Asian GPU. We take your great double popularity - as a major surgeon and a bishop - very much into account. We cannot allow you to continue your hunger strike. I give you my word of honour as a politician, that you will be released, if you stop your hunger strike." I said nothing. "Why don't you say anything? Do you not believe me?" I answered: "You know that I am a Christian, and the law of Christ tells us not to think wrongly about anyone. Very well, I'll believe you."
I was taken, not to the original place, but to a big empty hospital cell. The lock clanked, and I had the impression I was left alone. But suddenly I heard muffled, increasingly loud sobbing and I asked, "Who is crying? What are you crying about?" And I heard the following words, interrupted by sobs: "How can I not cry, when I see you? After all, we intensively follow your destiny already for a long time and we appreciate your

feat. I am a member of the central committee of the socialist-revolutionary party."

Before he could finish, the lock clanged and the chief of the secret department of the GPU entered the cell. He said to the social revolutionary that he would be taken to Samarkand, where he had been arrested, and there he would be released. Even this social revolutionary, who was experienced in the proceedings of the GPU, believed him. He had abstained from food already for the nineteenth day and he had come to the state of enfeeblement of the will to resist, of self-pity and fear of death, which are inevitable for those who are on hunger strike for a long time. For a few days they left him in Samarkand and, of course, he was not released but taken to Moscow. I do not know what happened to him further.

I, of course, was also not released, despite "the word of honour of a politician."

For two or three days I received plentiful parcels from my children, but then I refused them and resumed my hunger strike. It lasted for two weeks, and I got to the point that I could hardly walk through the hospital corridor, holding on to the wall. I tried to read the newspaper, but I did not understand anything, because it was as if a heavy shroud was lying on my brain.

Again the assistant chief of the secret department came to me and he said: "We have informed Moscow about your hunger strike and from there came a decision about your case, but we cannot make it known to you until you stop your hunger strike." There still glimmered in me a vestige of faith in the words of the Chekists, and I agreed to stop my hunger strike. Then I was told that I had to go to the city of Kotlas not as a transported convict, but freely. But also this time I was cheated. After about a week I was sent under escort.[90] We drove in a prisoner's carriage to Samara, where we were left in jail for about a week. The memories that have remained with me of this week are dark and heavy.

In Moscow I was put in another prisoner's carriage and the journey to the town of Kotlas continued. In the carriage there was such a great number of lice that in the morning and in the evening I took off all my underwear and every day I found in it hundreds of lice, among them were very large black lice I had never seen. On the way we each got a piece of bread and one raw herring for two. I did not eat them.

On arrival in Kotlas we were put over three versts away on the sandy shore of the Northern Dvina in a camp known as "Makarikha." It consisted of two hundred huts. Whole families of dispossessed kulaks[91] from many Russian provinces lived there. The boards of the gable roofs of the barracks started right in the sandy ground. Inside there were two rows of bunks and a middle passage. When it was raining streams of water poured into the barracks through the rotten roofs.

One morning I witnessed how two hundred prisoners were brought to the central yard of the camp and after registration they were forced on barges. The barges were pulled by a small steamer along the river Vychegda, a river flowing not far from Kotlas into the Northern Dvina.

The desolate Vychegda runs between dense uninhabited forests and, as I later learned, all those who were sent on barges were disembarked in the thick forest a few dozen versts from Kotlas. They were given axes and saws and they were ordered to build log cabins. I do not know what happened to them further. Soon I was transferred from Makarikha to Kotlas and I was allowed to receive patients at the outpatient clinic, but later I was transferred to work as a surgeon in the Kotlas hospital.

Before my transfer to Kotlas there was an outbreak of typhus in Makarikha. The Kotlas residents told me that a year ago in Makarikha also raged different kinds of typhus and epidemics of almost all infectious childhood diseases. In this terrible time each day in Makarikha a large hole was dug and at the end of the day about seventy corpses were buried in it.

I did not have to operate in the Kotlas hospital for very long. Soon I was notified that I had to go by boat to the city of Archangelsk. The first year of my life in Archangelsk I experienced great difficulties in terms of accommodation and I was almost homeless. Not only the doctors at the hospital, but, to my surprise, even the bishop of Archangelsk, met me in a quite unfriendly way.

I was given surgical work in a large clinic.[92] There I had the possibility to see insufficiently radical surgery for breast cancer of women, and therefore, when a patient with breast cancer came to me, I did not send her to the hospital, but decided to operate her ambulatory and I did a very radical operation. Learning about this, the hospital doctors went to complain about me to the head of the provincial health department, but he only asked them: "So, the operation was successful, the patient is alive, there are no complications? So what else do you need?"

While living in Archangelsk, I noticed I had a hard knobby tumour, which aroused the suspicion I had cancer and I reported this to the head of the secret department, asking for permission to travel to Moscow for an operation. He made a request to Moscow, and two weeks later I received permission to go to be operated, however not in Moscow but in Leningrad. I was surprised by this, but I took being sent to Leningrad as the path indicated to me by God.

In the train a young doctor got acquainted with me and upon arrival in Leningrad he invited me to stay with his family to save me from trouble in an unfamiliar city.

He took me far away to a large clinical hospital on Vasilievsky Island, to the surgical department of professor N.N. Petrov,[93] a prominent specialist in oncology. Professor Petrov treated me with great attention, and he operated me. The tumour that was cut out was non-malignant.

On discharge from the hospital, I went to the Novodevichy convent that had already been closed down, and I was very kindly received by metropolitan Seraphim, who lived there.

My former surgery student doctor Zholondz accompanied me from the clinic to the monastery. We spoke on medical topics, and I was very far from any mystical thoughts and moods. But here's what happened next: I came to the metropolitan on Saturday just before the evening service, and I made for the large monastery church in the most ordinary of moods. A hieromonk served, and I stood in the altar. When the time of reading the Gospel came near I suddenly felt an incomprehensible, very rapidly increasing emotion, which reached a great strength when I heard the reading. This was the eleventh Sunday Gospel reading. The words the Lord Jesus Christ addressed to saint Peter: "...Simon, son of Jonas, lovest thou me?... Feed my sheep,"[94] I perceived with unspeakable awe and emotion, as if they were not addressed to Peter, but directly to me. I was shaking all over, I could not wait until the end of the evening service, I went to metropolitan Seraphim, and told him what had happened. He listened with great interest to me and said that in his life similar things occurred. For another two to three months every time I thought about my experience when the eleventh Gospel was read, I started shaking again and tears would flow from my eyes.

Soon after my return from Leningrad to Archangelsk I was summoned to Moscow by the special commissioner of the collegium of the GPU, and on my arrival in Moscow, the commissioner spent three weeks talking with me for a long time every day. He was asked to review my case since according to him I was tried in Tashkent by "slow-witted dumbbells." It was clear that he was instructed to thoroughly examine me. In his words there was a lot of flattery, he praised me in every possible way. He promised me a surgical cathedra in Moscow, and it was quite clear that they wanted me to renounce serving as a priest.

As I said earlier, before my second arrest, I was allowed to retire by the patriarchal locum tenens metropolitan Sergius. Unnoticeably to me, the honeyed words of the special commissioner poisoned my heart, and a very grave misfortune and a great sin happened to me, for I wrote the following statement: "I am not employed as a bishop and I am retired. Under the present circumstances I do not consider it possible to continue serving, so if my priesthood permits it, I would like to have the opportunity to work as a surgeon. However, I will never discard the title of bishop."

I do not understand, I do not understand at all how I could so soon have forgotten the command of the Lord Jesus Christ Himself, that shook me so deeply in Leningrad: "Feed my lambs... Feed My sheep..." The only explanation I can find is that to break away from surgery was extremely difficult for me.

After my statement, a copy of which I sent to metropolitan Sergius, I was not only not released early, as happens with exiles who are called by the special commissioner, but I was returned to Archangelsk and another six months was added to the term of my exile.

Only at the end of 1933 was I released and I went to Moscow. It was of course known to the Lord God that I was taking a new gravely sinful step, and He warned me with a train accident, which, unfortunately, only scared me, and did not bring me to my senses. In Moscow, first thing I appeared in the chancellery of the locum tenens metropolitan Sergius. His secretary asked me if I wanted to take one of the vacant episcopal sees. Abandoned by God and devoid of reason, I deepened my grave sin by disobeying the command of Christ: "Feed My sheep," with the terrible answer: "No."

Somewhat earlier I had the intention to return to Tashkent and I wrote to metropolitan Arseny about it, but from his answer I understood that he would not be gladdened by my arrival at all.

Even before the end of my Archangelsk exile I had sent a letter to the healthcare commissar of Vladimir with the request to provide me with the opportunity to study in the special research institute for the development of purulent surgery. To my own ruin I set off from metropolitan Sergius to the ministry of healthcare to personally petition for it. The commissar of Vladimir did not receive me, and I went to his deputy. I asked the deputy to organize for me a special scientific research institute of purulent surgery. He had a very sympathetic attitude to my request and promised to talk about it with the director of the institute of experimental medicine, Fyodorov, who was soon to arrive. To the delight of the devil, to my ruin, I was very glad about this, but God protected me and directed my ways, kept me from downfall, because Fyodorov refused to grant a bishop the superintendence of a scientific research institute.

I had nowhere to go, but at a lunch at the home of metropolitan Sergius one of the bishops advised me to go to the Crimea. Without any rational aim I followed this advice and went to Feodosiya. There I felt I had lost the way and felt abandoned by God, ate in a dirty tavern, slept in a peasant's house, and finally took a new senseless decision - to return to Archangelsk. For over two months I again received patients in the ambulatory there. In Archangelsk a medical school opened at this time, and I was offered the cathedra of surgery. I refused, and coming to my senses a bit, I left for Tashkent.

But I could not stay in Tashkent and hinder metropolitan Arseny. I descended to such a level that I put on civilian clothes and in the ministry of health I was appointed consultant at the hospital of Andijan.

There I also felt that the grace of God had left me. My operations there were unsuccessful. I spoke as a lecturer about malignant formations, an inappropriate role for a bishop. Soon I was heavily punished by God. I was taken ill with tropical Pappataci fever, which was complicated by the retinal detachment of the left eye.

I left for Tashkent, and I was given the supervision of a little department of purulent surgery of twenty-five beds at the city hospital. Later, this department was expanded to fifty beds.

Soon I found out about the operations of the Swiss ophthalmologist Gonin[95] that cured 60-80% of patients with retinal detachment. This operation was soon widespread in many countries, and in Moscow it was done by professor Odintsov.[96] I left my work on purulent surgery and went to Moscow, to the clinic of Odintsov. He twice did the Gonin operation on me, because the first time he inaccurately identified all areas of retinal detachment. I was lying blindfolded after surgery, and late at night I was again suddenly seized with a longing to continue my work on purulent surgery. I was considering how to write to the health commissar again, and with these thoughts I fell asleep. To save me, the Lord God sent me a most unusual prophetic dream that I remember with perfect clarity to this day, after many years.

I dreamed I was in a small empty church, in which only the altar was brightly lit. In the church not far from the altar near the wall was the shrine of a saint, closed with a heavy wooden lid. In the altar on the throne was a wide board, with on it a naked human corpse. On the sides and behind the throne were students and doctors. Some smoked cigarettes and I read them a lecture about anatomy on the corpse. Suddenly I shuddered from a heavy knock and when I turned I saw that the cover had fallen from the shrine of the saint, he was sitting up in his coffin and turned to look at me in silent reproach. I woke up with terror...

It is incomprehensible to me that this terrible dream did not bring me to my senses. On being discharged from the hospital I returned to Tashkent,[97] and for two more years I continued to work in the purulent surgery department, a job that was often tied up with the necessity to conduct research on cadavers. And not once did I have the idea that such work is inadmissible for a bishop. For more than two years still I continued this work, and I could not put it down, because it allowed me one after the other, to make very important scientific discoveries, and the observations gathered in the purulent department were subsequently the major foundation for writing my book "Essays on purulent surgery."

In my penitential prayers I earnestly asked God's forgiveness for this two-year continuation of my work on surgery, but one day my prayer was stopped by a voice from the unearthly world: "Don't repent about this!" And I realized that "Essays on purulent surgery" had pleased God, for they greatly increased the power and significance of my confession of the name of Christ when anti-religious propaganda was in full swing.

On February 10th, 1936 metropolitan Arseny suddenly died of a brain hemorrhage. His eminence Arseny and I had a most close and friendly relationship. He loved my children and Sofia Sergeyevna and often visited them. He gave me two of his photographs, on one of them he wrote: "...be offered upon the sacrifice...",[98] and on the other: "...the bowels of the saints are refreshed by thee, brother."[99] He was photographed with me too. He listened very carefully to my sermons and he thought highly of them. Of himself he said that he had fulfilled all God had intended for him, and therefore he had awaited his death.

CHAPTER 7. THIRD ARREST

A year later, in 1937, began a terrible period for the holy church, the period of the rule of Yezhov as head of the Moscow GPU. Mass arrests of clergy and all those suspected of hostility to the Soviet authorities were started. Of course I was also arrested.[100] The Yezhov regime was truly terrible. During the interrogations the detainees were even tortured. The so-called interrogation conveyor was invented which twice I had to experience also. This terrible conveyor continued uninterruptedly day and night. The interrogating Chekists relieved each other, but the interrogated one was not allowed to sleep, day or night.
Again I started a hunger strike to protest and starved for days. Despite this, I was forced to stand in a corner, but I soon fell to the ground from exhaustion. I began to have pronounced visual and tactile hallucinations one after another. It seemed to me that yellow chickens were running around in the room and that I caught them. I saw myself standing on the edge of a vast pit, in which a whole town was located, brightly lit by electric lights. I clearly felt under my shirt on my back twisting snakes.
From me they relentlessly demanded a confession of espionage, but in return I asked them only to indicate, in the interest of which state I was spying. They couldn't, of course, answer that. The interrogation conveyor lasted for thirteen days, and more than once I was taken under the tap, from which they poured cold water over my head. Seeing no end to this interrogation, I decided to scare the Chekists. I demanded that they call the head of the secret department, and when he came, I said that I would sign all they wanted, except perhaps that I attempted to murder Stalin. I declared the termination of my hunger strike and asked them to send me lunch. I intended to slit my temporal artery by putting a knife to my temple and hitting hard on the back of the hilt. To stop the bleeding they would have to tie up the temporal artery, which is not feasible in the conditions of the GPU, and they would have to take me to a hospital or a surgical clinic. This would cause a scandal in Tashkent.

The next Chekist in turn sat down at the other end of the table. When they brought lunch, I inconspicuously touched the blunt blade of the table knife and I realized I would not succeed to cut my temporal artery with it. Then I jumped up and quickly ran to the middle of the room, and began to cut my throat with the knife. But I could not even cut my skin with it. The Chekist jumped on me like a cat, tore the knife out of my hands and punched me in the chest. I was taken to another room and they ordered me to sleep on a bare table with a bundle of newspapers under my head for a pillow. Despite the serious shock I had experienced, I fell asleep all the same, and I do not remember if I slept for long.

The chief of the secret department was already waiting for me to sign the lie that had been made up by him about my spying. I just laughed at this request.

Their nearly two-week conveyor had turned out to be a fiasco and I was returned to the basement of the GPU. I was totally exhausted by the hunger strike and the conveyor, and when we were released to the bathroom, I passed out on the dirty wet floor. They had to carry me to the cell. The next day I was taken in "a black raven" to the central provincial jail. There I spent about eight months in very difficult conditions.[101]

Our large cell was stuffed to excess with prisoners. They were lying on three-story bunks and on the stone floor in between. At night, when going to the close-stool which stood near the entrance, I had to make my way across the whole cell between the people lying on the floor, and I would stumble over them and fall on them.

Parcels were forbidden, and they fed us very badly. I still remember the lunch at the feast of the Annunciation of the most holy Mother of God, which consisted of a large tub of hot water, in which they had stirred a very little bit of buckwheat. I do not remember for what reason I got into the prison hospital. But with the help of God I was able to save the life of a young rogue there, who was seriously ill. I saw that the young prison doctor did not understand his illness at all. I examined him and found a splenic abscess. I managed to get the consent of the prison doctor to send this patient to the clinic where my student, doctor Rothenberg worked. I wrote to him how to operate and what he would find when operating, and Rothenberg later wrote that everything described in my letter proved correct word for word.

The life of the rogue was saved, and for a long time after that during our airings in the prison yard, criminal prisoners greeted me loudly from the third floor and thanked me for saving the life of the rogue.

Unfortunately, I have forgotten much of what I lived through in the provincial jail. I only remember that I was taken to new interrogations in the GPU and they strove more intensely to achieve my confession of some espionage. The interrogation conveyor was repeated. Once the Chekist conducting it fell asleep. The chief of the secret department came in and woke him up. The Chekist who had got in trouble had always been very polite to me, but now he began to kick my legs with his feet which were clad in leather boots. Soon after that, when I was already exhausted by the interrogation conveyor, I sat with my head low down. I saw that facing me there stood three main Chekists watching me. By their order I was taken to the basement of the GPU and I was put in a very cramped punishment cell. The escorting soldiers who changed my clothes saw the very large bruises on my legs and asked how I got them. I replied that I was kicked by some Chekist. In the basement I was tortured in solitary confinement for several days in very difficult conditions. Later I learned that the results of my first interview on espionage were reported to the Moscow GPU. There they were found to be unsuitable, and it was ordered to hold a new investigation. Evidently, this explains my long imprisonment in the provincial jail and the second questioning by interrogation conveyor.

Although this second investigation was also inconclusive, I was still sent on a third exile to Siberia for three years.

This time they took me, not through Moscow, but through Almaty and Novosibirsk. On the road to Krasnoyarsk I was robbed on the train in a mean way by rogues. In front of the eyes of all the prisoners a young rogue sat down next to me.

He said he was the son of a Leningrad prosecutor and for a long time "he drew the wool over my eyes," while behind me two other rogues emptied my suitcase.

In Krasnoyarsk they kept us not for long in some forwarding prison on the outskirts of the city and from there they took us to the village of Bolshaya Murtha,[102] about 150 kilometers from Krasnoyarsk. There I lived at first in poverty without permanent accommodation, but soon I was given a room at the district hospital and they provided me with work in it together with the doctor of that place and his wife, also a physician. Later they told me that I had barely been able to walk from weakness after the very bad food in the Tashkent prison, and they thought I was a decrepit old man. But pretty soon I became stronger and developed an extensive surgical practice at the Murtha hospital.

From Tashkent they sent me a lot of case histories from the purulent department of the Tashkent hospital, and thanks to this I had the opportunity to write many chapters of my book "Essays on purulent surgery."

Unexpectedly I was called to the Murtha GPU, and to my surprise they announced that I was allowed to go to the city of Tomsk to work in the very extensive library of the medical faculty there. One might think that this was the result of the request I had sent sent from the Tashkent prison to marshal Kliment Voroshilov[103] to give me the opportunity to finish my work on purulent surgery, which would be indispensable for military surgery.

In Tomsk, I settled in a large apartment, given by a deeply religious woman. In two months I managed to re-read the latest literature on purulent surgery in German, French and English, and I copied big extracts from it. On my return to Murtha I had fully completed my big book "Essays on purulent surgery."

The summer of 1941[104] set in when Hitler's hordes, having done with the Western countries, invaded the Soviet Union. At the end of July the chief surgeon of the Krasnoyarsk province arrived by plane in Bolshaya Murtha. He asked me to fly with him to Krasnoyarsk, where I was appointed chief surgeon of evacuation hospital 15-15.[105] This hospital was accommodated on three floors of a large building formerly occupied by a school. There I worked for at least two years, and the memories remaining of this work are bright and joyful.

The wounded officers and soldiers loved me a lot.[106] When I went around the wards in the morning, I was cheerfully greeted by the wounded. Some of them had been unsuccessfully operated on injured large joints in other hospitals. If they were cured by me they invariably saluted me with a straight leg raised high.

At the end of the war I wrote a moderately sized book "Late resections on infected wounds of large joints," which I presented to be nominated for the Stalin Prize along with the big book "Essays on purulent surgery."

At the end of working in evacuation hospital 15-15 I received a letter of acknowledgment of the West Siberian military district, and at the end of the war I was awarded a medal "For valiant labour in the great patriotic war of 1941-1945."

The holy synod under the locum tenens of the patriarchal throne, metropolitan Sergius, equated my medical treatment of the wounded to valiant episcopal ministry, and raised me to the rank of archbishop.

In Krasnoyarsk I combined treating the wounded with episcopal ministry in the eparchy of Krasnoyarsk and on all Sundays and holidays I walked far out of the city to a small graveyard church, because there was no other church in Krasnoyarsk. I had to walk through such mud that once I got stuck halfway, and fell in the mud, and had to return home.

Serving the episcopal rite was impossible, since there was no one with me, except for one old priest, so I limited myself to only zealously preaching the word of God.

At the end of my exile in 1943 I returned to Moscow and was appointed to Tambov.[107] In this province before the revolution there had been a hundred and ten churches and I found only two: in Tambov and in Michurinsk. Having a lot of free time, for two years I combined church service and work in hospitals for the wounded in Tambov also.

In 1946 I was awarded the Stalin prize first class for my "Essays on purulent surgery" and "Late resections on infected wounds of large joints."[108]

In May 1946 I was appointed archbishop of Simferopol and Crimea.[109] The student youth had come to the station to meet me with flowers, but the reception did not not take place as I arrived by airplane. That was on May 26th, 1946.

Here the memoirs stop abruptly. They were dictated to secretary E.P. Leykfeld by archbishop Luke in 1958 in Simferopol. He was completely blind then. Archbishop Luke died on June 11th, 1961. He is buried in Simferopol, where he held the cathedra for fifteen years. [ed.]

APPENDICES

The memory of archbishop Luke (Voyno-Yasenetsky)

Each one of the clergy of our church considered it a great honour to have communion with archbishop Luke, to receive his blessing, to perform the divine Liturgy with him. I would like to share my memories of meeting vladyko, which occurred in Alushta by a fortunate circumstance.

In 1958 the late bishop Innokenty[110] of Kirovograd was appointed to attend an episcopal consecration in Odessa. I accompanied him to Odessa as an eparchial secretary. The Divine Liturgy was led by the most holy patriarch Alexy. On the same day the most holy patriarch sent bishop Innokenty to Simferopol to archbishop Luke for church affairs. We already knew that vladyko Luke, who before did not see with one eye, had become blind also in his second eye.

The next morning we arrived in Simferopol in our eparchial car. It was the day before the Transfiguration of the Lord. We did not find vladyko at home. He was at the small dacha which he rented in the town of Alushta. In the bishop's house we were offered a cup of tea to refresh ourselves. His eminence Luke occupied a very modest apartment on the second floor. It consisted of two small rooms. One room was the episcopal cell, the second served as reception room, dining room and office. The walls were filled from floor to ceiling by shelves with books, the personal library of the archbishop.

After tea we went to Alushta, where in the country by the sea was the small house where vladyko Luke spent the summers. The apartment here consisted also of two small rooms. I remember that the modest lunch and dinner were served in the open air in the small front garden. Archbishop Luke lived in Alushta with one person who served him. His eparchial secretary came to report every other day. Vladyko examined all eparchial questions very thoroughly. We were present at the time of such a report, and we were surprised at the memory of his eminence Luke and how well he was informed, his practical aptitude and extraordinary ability to make the right decision.

We immediately noted that archbishop Luke walked around the apartment, the house and the front garden without a stick. He fetched the things he needed himself, rearranged the plates, served himself from the dishes, took the books he needed from the shelves, etc. He questioned bishop Innokenty in detail about the Kirovograd eparchy, about our trip to Odessa, about the ministry of the most holy patriarch and about the consecration that had taken place.

When he was living in Alushta vladyko Luke already no longer received patients. As a doctor he was a keen diagnostician and he could accurately determine the outcome of a disease. We were told that local clinics sometimes sent the most severely ill patients to the blind professor, archbishop Luke, for him to make the correct diagnosis. Once some parents took their sick son to vladyko. Vladyko probed him and correctly identified the illness. Then he asked to take the son out of the room. He waited for the parents and told them: "Place your trust in the Lord, I must tell you the truth: before ten days have passed, your son will pass away from you to the heavenly abodes." Everything happened as vladyko Luke predicted.

In the evening of August 18th, we went to the all-night vigil in the church of the city of Alushta. A solemn celebration with two bishops was arranged. Vladyko Luke was not taken by the arm to lead his way. He was apparently guided by the sound of the steps of bishop Innokenty. He received the holy cross from the rector of the church and then archbishop Luke gave it to his eminence Innokenty to kiss, and then to us, the priests and deacons.

The solemn vigil began. Vladyko Luke said the prayers of light in a low voice from memory, though in front of him a service book was held in which he sometimes moved his fingers under the lines. For the litany bishop Innokenty came out and for the polyeleos both bishops. The censing of the whole church was done by archbishop Luke, who was supported by a subdeacon on the steps and at some of the turns in the church. The Gospel of the feast was also read by vladyko Luke. He read without mistakes. From time to time he ran his finger along the text, which was not protuberant, as books for the blind are printed, but usual. Bishop Innokenty anointed the parishioners with consecrated oil, but the clerics were anointed by archbishop Luke. He touched each lightly and anointed everyone accurately in the middle of the brow.

During the vigil bishop Luke listened carefully to every word, every chant. He was completely absorbed in prayer and with his spirit he stood not on earth, but in heaven before the throne of God.

In the morning the archpastors arrived at the church to serve the Divine Liturgy. The church was filled with believers, many of whom were health-resort visitors. Like the day before, vladyko Luke came out of the car himself, unaided, and walked to the entrance of the church. He firmly treaded over the path that had been rolled out for him, then he listened and read the entrance prayers, kissed the icons. Those who did not know about the blindness of vladyko, could not have imagined that the Divine Liturgy was performed by an archpastor blind in both eyes. Archbishop Luke cautiously touched the diskos with his hand , correctly blessed the holy sacraments during their transubstantiation, he did not brush against them with either his hands or vestments. All prayers of the mystery vladyko said from memory and only in two cases he did he run his finger along the text of the service book. Vladyko partook of holy communion himself and administered communion to the clerics. We looked at it all as a manifestation of God's guidance that makes the blind see.

Archbishop Luke folded the holy antimins himself and ended the service of the Liturgy. Before the dismissal he came out to preach the sermon. The whole church stood stock-still in expectation. And here the preacher opened his mouth. He told the story of the feast of the Transfiguration of the Lord. His eminence Luke spoke further about the illumination of believers by divine light, as on Tabor. The archbishop emphasized that a believer, who is devoted to God and who loves Him, cannot be blind, because he is illuminated by a special light of God, which gives him a special vision, a special joy in the Lord Jesus Christ. Archbishop Luke underpinned his sermon with texts of the holy Scripture, he mentioned certain books, chapters and verses, which the rector, who was standing next to vladyko, read aloud. Every word of the preacher came from his heart, every word was full of deep faith and devotion to God's will. From all sides in the church were heard tears and quiet sobs. The archbishop's words fell like ripe seeds deeply into the hearts of the listeners. Everyone felt renewed after a sermon of such strength of spirit and faith.

We were in Alushta with archbishop Luke for one more day, August 20th, after which our stay with our hospitable host in Alushta was over.

Archpriest Eugene Vorshevsky, Cherkasy

EINDNOTES

[Additions by editors in square brackets]

1   "Valentin Felixovich Voyno-Yasenetsky, nobleman of orthodox religious persuasion, born in 1877 (April 14th) in the city of Kerch. Received his secondary education in the 2nd Chisinau and 2nd Kiev gymnasiums..." That is what's indicated in the resume that comes with the dissertation of V.F. Voyno-Yasenetsky, "Local anesthesia," 1915. [P.]
2   On Good Friday. [tr.]
3   Viktor Mikhaylovich Vasnetsov (1848-1926) specialized in mythological subjects. He is considered the co-founder of Russian folklorist and romantic modernist painting. [tr.]
4   Mikhail Vasilyevich Nesterov (1862-1942) was a major representative of religious symbolism in Russian art. [tr.]
5   At that time Valentin Voyno-Yasenetsky wrote a letter to Leo Tolstoy. It was published in "Herald of the Russian Christian movement" № 170 (III - 1994). [P.]
6   The editor's note has been moved to endnote xx. [tr.]
7   Mt. 9:37-38. [ed.]
8   Now called biochemistry.
9   Blindness was a great scourge in some provinces of Russia. The Russian village with its filth and poverty had from time immemorial been a hotbed of trachoma. Many victims of this blinding disease were asking for alms on the road.
Because he intended to become a country doctor, Voyno-Yasenetsky did not forget about this national curse. In the autumn of 1903, immediately after graduation from the university, he started visiting an eye clinic in Kiev. It seemed to him there were not enough appointments and operations in the clinic, and he began to receive patients at home. "Our apartment," recalls vladyko Luke's sister Victoria, "became for a time an eye infirmary. There were patients lying in the rooms, like in hospital wards. Valentin treated them, and my mother nursed them." This Kiev experience proved very useful to him later in country hospitals. In Ardatov and Lyubazh the reputation the new doctor earned with eye operations grew so swiftly that

the surgeon did not have time to examine all those wishing to have surgery. [P.]
10   Chita is the administrative center of Zabaykalsky province, nine hundred kilometres east of Irkutsk. [tr.]
11   Felix Lejars (1863-1932). [tr.]
12   Anna Vasilyevna Lanskaya. [P.]
13   Now republic of Mordovia, a federal subject of Russia. [tr.]
14   Ophthalmology is a branch of medicine that studies eye diseases. [ed.]
15   Heinrich Friedrich Wilhelm Braun (1862-1934). [tr.]
16   One method of local anesthesia is based on the interruption of the conductivity of nerve tubes that transfer pain sensitivity from the area that is subject to surgery. With one injection, the surgeon reaches full anesthesia of a large area of the body. [P.]
17   Tracheotomy consists in making an incision in the front of the neck and thereby opening a direct airway into the trachea. The resulting stoma can serve independently as an airway or as a place for a tracheostomy tube to be inserted. [ed.]
18   Associated with the "bison" from Kursk, Nikolai Yevgenyevich Markov, a right wing political figure. [tr.]
19   Nationalist movement. [tr.] The editors tried as much as possible to preserve the original text of the memories. But they do not necessarily share the views of the author. [ed.]
20   A letter to his wife speaks of the work attitude of the future archbishop Luke: "I do not want to leave Moscow before I have taken from it what I need: knowledge and the ability to work scientifically. As usual I work beyond measure and I am already heavily overworked... But there is a big job to be done: for the thesis I must learn French and German and read about five hundred works in French and German. In addition, I have to work a lot on my doctoral exams... In any case, I cannot become a doctor of medicine earlier than towards January 1910, if I will be free of all kinds of other activities all the time. But after that there will be a wide road open for me..." [P.]
21   Fyodor Aleksandrovich Rein (1866-1925). [tr.]
22   When he was engaged in scientific research vladyko Luke always had vital goals. He was guided by the desire to al-

leviate the suffering of patients and the labour of physicians. In those years general anesthesia was very imperfect and with the words of doctor Voyno-Yasenetsky often "incomparably more dangerous than the operation itself," and to use such a precise method of local pain relief as local anesthesia was a huge practical necessity, especially for district physicians. Surgery had a tremendous significance for vladyko Luke because with surgery he could serve poor and suffering people. In 1908-1909 in the journal "Surgery" appeared the first scientific works of V.F. Voyno-Yasenetsky on issues of pain relief. In only twelve years, the first twelve of his surgical occupation, the future vladyko Luke published nineteen of his forty-two scientific works. [P.]

23   *But I had nothing to live from in Moscow with a wife and two young children, so I left to work in a twenty-five bed hospital in Romanovka village in Balashov district in Saratov province...*

Romanovka was an extensive steppe village on the river Khopyor, with two churches and four taverns. On no matter what holiday, on the broad streets of Romanovka there would begin drinking bouts, brawls and knife-fights. According to the stories of the old medic Victor Fedosevich Elatomiev, who worked in the Romanovka settlement soon after Voyno-Yasenetsky, diseases also gained immense scale there: domestic syphilis - the whole village could have it, "pneumonia - such that could be seen from a distance, phlegmon - with half a bucket of pus." Two physicians, three nurses and a paramedic working without a moment's respite for days on end could hardly cope with the influx of patients. Between hundred and hundred and fifty people would come to the clinic at consultation hour. And after that he had to go around the villages on horseback or in a cart. There were plenty of cases there too because there were twenty villages and twelve hamlets in the locality. There, on the spot, he had to do operations under narcosis, apply forceps in childbirth.

This is how the country hospital in Romanovka is presented in "A survey of the state of country medicine in Balashov district in 1907-1910 and part of 1911": "Locality Romanovka. Area five hundred and eighty square versts. Population thirty to five hundred and six people. More than seventy percent of the population is located more than eight versts from the house of the doctor. Clinic – thirty one to six hundred and forty consultations a year. The area of the locality is twice the required norm and the population and the amount of work three times." Because twnty five to thirty patients had to be received in an hour, each could be given no more than two minutes for examination as well as prescription. Consultation went on for five to seven hours a day. According to estimates of the compiler of "A survey": "...Only in forty five cases out of a hundred a roughly accurate diagnosis can be given, but fifty five go through without a diagnosis. The share one doctor had to take was often up to two hundred people... The facilities for the reception of outpatients are for the most part crowded and stuffy. In the Balashov locality for example, in one room three doctors receive patients, two of them sit behind one desk. In the same room behind a screen there are gynecological examinations, next door in the dressing room they are making incisions, vaccinations for children. All this is accompanied by screaming, crying. The waiting rooms are jammed and noisy. There are cases of fainting from lack of air. Listening with a stethoscope is out of the question." In these cramped, stuffy and noisy conditions Valentin Felixovich worked for a year and a half. In addition to consultations and visits he also had to do all surgery in the hospital. "I did no less than three hundred operations a year in Romanovka," he writes in his resumé in 1945. "A survey" confirms that in 1909 the surgeon carried out two hundred and ninety two surgeries. In the beginning of the next year, the operational tempo increased even more... [P.]

24   Pyotr Ivanovich Karuzin (1864-1939). [tr.]
25   Circular hole (Latin). [ed.]
26   *By the end of this work I... occupied the position of chief physician and surgeon of a fifty beds district hospital in Pereslavl.*
The Pereslavl hospital differed little from the one in Romanovka: there was neither electricity nor an X-ray machine, the water was delivered by the water carrier in a barrel, and almost daily the life of the hospital was paralyzed for a few hours when they were cleaning the smelly pit which replaced the sewage system. The hospital served as the center of medical care for the whole district, so it was mostly neighbouring farmers who flocked to see a doctor at consultation hours.

At half past eight in the morning the hospital coachman Alexander used to drive up to the house of the chief physician with a carriage. The Voyno-Yasenetskys occupied a quite spacious wooden house of lady landowner Lileyevaya at Trinity Street, near the place where now the highway Moscow-Yaroslavl cuts through an ancient earthen rampart. The distance from the house to the hospital was not more than a verst, but also this time the doctor did not pass in vain. In the carriage he took with him fifteen to twenty cards with German and French words, and learned them on the road.

The eldest son of vladyko Luke, Mikhail Valentinovich, recalling that time, tells: "My father worked during the day, evening, night. In the morning we did not see him, he left for the hospital early. We had dinner together, but father also remained silent then, he mostly read a book at the table. Mother tried not to distract him. She was also not loquacious."

The former housemaid who served the Voyno-Yasenetskys for seven years, Elizabeth Nikanorovna Kokina, remembers them with love:

Anna Vasilyevna was the most attractive woman of the whole town. Of large stature, stout, but she tired quickly. But how could she not get tired? To clothe and feed six is no joke. It was not like now: you couldn't go and buy at the store all you needed.

She loved her husband to the point of forgetting everything else. She did not contradict him in anything. Maybe there were some disagreements between them, but not when the children or servants were present, not for the life of one. The master was severe. He didn't touch household matters. He never said an unnecessary word. If at dinner he did not like something, he would get up and leave without a word. And Anna Vasilyevna then looked at her plate: "What was not to his liking there?"

At eight in the morning the master had breakfast alone. He came to dinner at five. After dinner he had a little rest. Later he received patients in the study and after the evening samovar he withdrew to his study. He was writing there, reading, until all kerosene in the lamp had burned up. He was often called to the hospital at night. He would pack his things without a word and leave. He never got angry when they called...

"He was righteous," repeated Elizabeth Nikanorovna several times, and she continues:
They lived quietly. Once a month their acquaintance the hegumena of the Feodorov monastery came to drink a cup of tea. She was a woman of great mind. Yes, also doctor Mikhnevich with his wife Sofia Mikhailovna would drop in. They worked together at the hospital.
With the children the master and mistress were very tender. They did not punish them, did not even say rough words . Mother only put Misha sometimes in the storeroom because of his pranks. But she let him out soon.
Mikhail Valentinovich did not remember about the storeroom, but the gentle benevolent tone accepted in the family deeply imprinted itself in his memory. "The furniture in the Pereslavl house was nothing to look at to the last degree," he says. "Father did not have savings, neither then, nor later." E.N. Kokina speaks about this too: "They, the Yasenetskys, had nothing to show off with. They kept no wine or tobacco in the house. Sweets, also, were never there. Only books, they were sent to him by post. There were many books. They went neither to theaters, nor on visits, and they were rarely visited..." [P.]

27   Alexei Vasilyevich Martynov (1868-1934). [tr.]

28   *In Tashkent... I often had to scrub the floors myself because of the disarray of life which is inevitable during a revolution.*
By the end of 1917 the situation in Tashkent had sharply deteriorated. Products became more expensive, the bazaars were deserted, the maid of the Voyno-Yasenetskys would spend the time from early morning to midafternoon standing in queues. Bullets were whistling over the hospital yard. The walls of the buildings got covered with bullet scars like smallpox. During one of these exchanges of fire, operation sister Sofia Sergeyevna Beletskaya was wounded in the thigh. Another time a bullet whizzed by the very ear of the head physician.
Professor of anthropology Lev Vasilyevich Oshanin worked for three years as a doctor in the hospital in Tashkent under the direction of Voyno-Yasenetsky. With deep respect for Valentin Felixovich he recalls in his manuscript "Essays on the History of the medical community in Tashkent":

It was an anxious time. We were on twenty-four hour duty every two or three days. In 1917-1920 it was dark in the city. At night There was constant shooting on the streets. Who and why they were shooting, we did not know. But the wounded were taken to hospital. I am not a surgeon and except for easy cases I always called Voyno-Yasenetsky to decide whether to keep the patient bandaged overnight or to operate immediately. At any hour of the night, he would immediately get dressed and be under way to my call. Sometimes the wounded came in one after another. Often they were operated immediately, so that the night would pass without sleep. It happened that Voyno-Yasenetsky was called at night to the house of the patient or to another hospital for a consultation, or for an urgent surgery. He set out at once for such nightly, unsafe (as robberies were frequent) trips. Just as immediately and smoothly Voyno-Yasenetsky would come when you called him to the medical department for a consultation. On his face there never was an expression of annoyance or dissatisfaction that he was being disturbed for trifles (from the point of view of an experienced surgeon). On the contrary, you could feel his complete readiness to help.

I never saw him angry, inflamed or simply irritated. He always spoke calmly, in a low voice, unhurriedly, low-key. He never raised his voice. This does not mean that he was indifferent – a lot of things roused his indignation, but he never lost his temper, and his indignation was expressed in the same quiet voice.

The health of Anna Vasilyevna deteriorated, her nerves were always strained. By the winter food became altogether sparse. Anna could somehow walk around the house, but she could not cook or clean up. The children remember how Valentin Felixovich scrubbed the floors in the evening. He wrapped old bandages around a broom. They began to deliver dinner from the hospital kitchen - rotten sauerkraut in muddy water. Doctor Moses Slonim treated Anna Vasilyevna. He was the best physician of the city, he treated dignitaries and had a private practice. He was a good man, he tried to support the sick Anna not only with medicine, but also with nourishing food: the doctor sent from his own table dinners that were rather abundant for the time. Also the family of surgeon Rothenberg sent food to Anna. They kept it secret from Voyno-Yasenetsky. But neither Slonim's dinners, nor the Rothenbergs's food brought much benefit. Anna gave the food away to the children, and she was eating the same cabbage soup as her husband. Her health was finally undermined by the arrest of Valentin Felixovich during the uprising of the Turkestan regiment. [P.]

29   K. Osipov, defense commissar of the republic of Turkestan, attempted in January 1919 to seize power in Tashkent. Whether it was directed against Bolshevik excesses or Osipov simply deliberated to appoint himself dictator is unknown, but during the suppression of the uprising a lot of innocent people suffered. [P.]

30   ...*we met workers on the road. They were extremely surprised that we had been released from the workshops.*

Professor Oshanin told the following about the arrest of Voyno-Yasenetsky:

The chief physician was arrested along with his closest student surgeon R.A. Rothenberg by a patrol of two workers and two sailors. The patrolmen were led to the surgical department by morgue attendant Andrey, a drunkard and a thief, whom Voyno-Yasenetsky for all his patience, had long since promised to dismiss from work. The news that Valentin Felixovich had been taken to the railway workshops provoked people to be in very low spirits at the hospital. The workshops had a terrible reputation. The very phrase: "Take him to the railway workshops" meant in those days nothing other than: "Shoot him." It all happened in the early morning and until late into the night nobody knew anything about the fate of those arrested. Rothenberg returned, accompanied by two armed workers. He gave a detailed account of what had happened. At the workshops they were put in a very large room. There were many others who were arrested. One door led to the room where "the Cheka trio" was in session. Cases were usually solved quickly. Few came back from the trial. Most convicts (to sort out the fate of each, the "judges" did not spend more than three minutes) were led away through another door. The sentence was to be executed immediately. The two doctors sat in front of the fateful door for more than half an hour. All this time Voyno-Yasenetsky remained perfectly calm. To the frequent anxious questions of Rothenberg:

"Why don't they call us? What may that mean?" Valentin Felixovich answered, "They will call us when the time will come, sit quietly." Late in the evening a prominent party member walked through the "hall of death." He knew the chief physician by sight. He was surprised to see the famous surgeon here and asked what had happened. Then he disappeared into the court room. Ten minutes later, the doctors were given permits to go back to the hospital. But the party member who helped them would not let them go alone. The situation in the city was too tense: the medics could be killed by any patrol they met, notwithstanding the stamp of "the trio."

The news that the arrested had returned, quickly spread all over the hospital. The doctors and nurses came running to the staff room, everyone wanted to see with his own eyes that the doctor was alive. However, Voyno-Yasenetsky prevented them. He asked not only to refrain from all ovations, but in general from any emotional outbursts. At the usual morning hour appointed for operation a patient was prepared, cleaned and taken to the operating room. All were at their places. Exactly on time, to the minute, the surgeon came to the operating table, and began to work with a scalpel as if nothing had happened. [P.]

31   Ps. 112:3. [ed.]
32   Ps. 112:9. [ed.]
33   Sofia Sergeyevna's husband was a tsar's officer and he was killed at the front. There is a picture of the surgical nurse with her colleagues in the operating room. On it we see a thin woman of about forty. She has a lively face, full of goodwill and sympathy. She was a genuine nurse, of the old school. In the operating room she was appreciated for her skill and modesty: without superfluous words she immediately guessed what tool a surgeon would require the next moment...

Sofia Sergeyevna died in the house of Valentin Voyno-Yasenetsky, the youngest son of vladyko Luke. She lived to a great age. [P.]

34   Before beginning an operation the future vladyko Luke would always make the sign of the cross and pray with concentration. He would turn towards the icon of the Mother of God, which hung in the operating room of the city hospital for many years. Irreligious doctors stopped paying attention

to it, and the religious regarded it as a most common matter. In the early twenties one of the inspection committees ordered to remove the icon. In response to this Valentin Felixovich left the hospital and said he would return only after the icon was returned to its place. According to the memoirs of professor L.V. Oshanin, the commission spoke out to make the point that "the operating room is a state institution. In our country the church is separated from the state. If your surgeon wants to pray, let him pray, no one will prevent him, but let him keep the icon at home." Voyno-Yasenetsky repeated that he wouldn't return to the operating room. But at this time a major party figure brought his wife to the hospital for an urgent surgery. The woman categorically declared that she wished to be operated by Voyno-Yasenetsky. "He was called to the reception," writes professor Oshanin. "He was sorry, but he confirmed that according to his religious beliefs, he wouldn't go into the operating room until the icon was hung back... The man who had brought the patient stated that he gave 'his word of honour' that the icon would be in place tomorrow if only the doctor immediately operated the patient. Voyno-Yasenetsky immediately went to the surgical unit and operated on the woman who subsequently fully recovered. The next morning, the icon really did hang in the operating room." [P.]

35   The Living church, also called Renovationist church, was a schism in the Russian orthodox church in 1922–1946. Originally begun as a movement among the Russian clergy for the reformation of the church, it was corrupted by the Soviet secret services, who hoped to split the Russian church. [tr.]

36   Innokentiy, in the world Alexander Dmitriyevich Pustynsky (1868-1937).

37   The choice of the priesthood by father Valentin was received with hostility by all his colleagues. Young students dared to make comments and "expose" the surgeon-priest. In response to this, remembers professor Z.I. Umidova, he only smiled indulgently. On the first day father Valentin came to the hospital in a cassock, his pupil A.I. Benyaminovich said: "I am not a believer, and whatever you may concoct, I'll just call you by your name and patronymic. For me father Valentin does not exist." [P.]

38   *...in Tashkent I was one of the initiators of founding the university... I was... selected for the cathedra of topographical anatomy and operative surgery...*

Tashkent university opened in the autumn of 1920. Having become a professor, Valentin Felixovich had to labour every day even more. He thoroughly prepared his lectures, without regard to his rest and quiet. At the same time other people turned the life of citizens into a meaningless and unbearable nightmare.

In Tashkent raged malaria, cholera, typhus. Famine around the Volga drove starving masses to Turkestan. They lay side by side at the station: in ragged clothes, covered with lice. Walking to the sub-faculty the professor would come across carts loaded with naked corpses. They were being carried out of the typhus department that was packed beyond every measure. Sick people and corpses were even lying at the hospital gates. Before the endless stream of sufferers the doctors became discouraged. The authorities continued the massacre they had started in '17 and there was no end in sight.

All around Turkestan they searched and caught those who had had anything to do with the former system: major and minor officials of the tsarist administration, members of the city council and officers. For "the previous" there was no excuse. They were shot without a trial. A general who showed his total contempt for his persecutors was shot dead in his prison cell... through the spyhole. The newspapers wrote about it as an everyday event.

Valentin Felixovich was ordained a priest. As professor Oshanin recalls, father Valentin "walked around the city in a cassock and with a cross and so he made the Tashkent authorities very nervous. He was by that time the chief physician of the city hospital, generally acknowledged first surgeon, chairman of the union of physicians. He lectured at the university with the cross on his chest. He lectured well, the students loved him, although they were rather afraid of him. Apart from operations and teaching Voyno-Yasenetsky was much engaged in painting: he painted icons for the church and anatomical tables for his university lessons. The authorities tolerated this for long, although they tried to persuade him to leave his church activities. He did not give in, however." And in the hospital the main surgeon blessed the patients before surgery.

Those who thought Voyno-Yasenetsky was "lost for science" were probably baffled when they met father Valentin at the first scientific congress of Turkestan doctors in Tashkent in 1922. The priest-surgeon delivered four big papers and took the floor in debates ten times, because of his great scientific and practical experience.

Many doctors told me that father Valentin treated every sick person always with great love and great attention, that his attitude to the sick "was ideal." [P.]

39   1 Cor. 1:17,31. [ed.]

40   *His eminence Innokentiy rarely preached. He appointed me as fourth priest of the cathedral and charged me with all preaching work. Giving me the task, he said to me with the words of apostle Paul: "Your job is 'not to baptize, but to preach'."*

In the summer of 1921 father Valentin had to publicly appear in court. Professor Oshanin recalls: "One day a group of wounded red army men was brought to Tashkent from Bukhara. On the way, they had been bandaged in the hospital train. But it was summertime, and under the bandages were growing larvae of flies... The wounded were placed in the clinic of professor Sitkovsky. The working day was over, and the doctors left. The doctor on duty applied two or three urgent dressings and the rest of the wounded he just quickly bandaged and he left them to be treated radically in the morning. Immediately out of nowhere the rumour spread that the clinic doctors were engaged in subversive activity, that they left wounded soldiers, whose wounds are swarming with worms, to rot."

Then at the head of the Cheka was the Latvian Peters. In the city he had a menacing reputation of relentless cruelty and he was very fast with pronouncing a "capital offence" sentence. On his order professor P.P. Sitkovsky and all the physicians of the clinic were arrested and imprisoned. Also two or three doctors who worked for the healthcare commissariat were arrested.

Peters decided to hold a show trial. Like the majority of Latvians from the Cheka, he spoke Russian badly, but, despite this, he appointed himself public prosecutor. In this role he pronounced a not too eloquent but "thunderous" indictment. In the speech there was mention of "White Guard chaff" and "counter-revolution" and "a clear betrayal." The accused were threatened with execution.

"Other speeches I do not remember," writes professor Oshanin, "except the statement of professor Voyno-Yasenetsky, who was summoned with a number of other expert surgeons... He fearlessly attacked the terrifying Peters straight away. He literally thrashed Peters as a gross ignoramus who undertakes to judge things he does not understand and as an unscrupulous demagogue who demands capital punishment for completely honest and conscientious people." Professor S.A. Masumov recalls the following about the trial:

The courtroom was full. Most of all there were workers, but the doctors of the city received some number of passes. By order of Peters professor Sitkovsky was brought from jail to the courtroom by horse guards. The professor walked in the middle of the street with his hands behind his back. By his sides clattered the hooves of the horses of his escort who rode with drawn swords. The trial was needed for "educational" purposes, to better show the working class its enemies, the servants of world capitalism. But the magnificently conceived and staged performance went down the drain when the president of the court called as an expert professor Voyno-Yasenetsky.

"Priest and professor Voyno-Yasenetsky," Peters addressed himself to father Valentin, "do you believe that professor Sitkovskiy is guilty of the scandalous practices, which were found in his clinic?"

The question concerned the first of the charges. The head of the clinic was accused of defective discipline among patients and staff. The wounded lying in the hospital drank, fought and took whores into the wards, and the doctors and nurses allegedly showed indulgence for this.

"Mister public prosecutor," the answer of expert Voyno-Yasenetsky came, "I request to also arrest me for the same reason. For my clinic also is in such a mess as the one of professor Sitkovskiy."

"Do not hurry, the time will come when we will arrest you!" yelled Peters.

In the surgical clinics of the city terrible practices were in fact going on. Most of the wounded lying in the clinics of professors Sitkovskiy, Voyno-Yasenetsky and Borowski were red army men. The large halls for one formation in the former military high school had been turned into wards. The appetite of the lads had grown at the fronts, so in those halls they drank home brew nonstop, smoked tobacco and publicly engaged in lechery. Right beside them were lying seriously injured people. But to their pleas for peace and quiet the lightly wounded did not pay any attention. Once, when the professor made his round, resident doctor Benyaminovich reported to him about yet another orgy that had taken place in a ward.

Valentin Felixovich ordered to call the rowdies to see him. But he had hardly reached the second floor to go to his office when a whole gang of drunken red army men appeared at the bottom of the stairs. Then they climbed the stairs to "beat the priest." Doctor Benyaminovich managed to lock herself in the operating room, but the professor was beaten up. They beat brutally. They kicked with their legs and crutches. After these beatings the head of the clinic was bedridden for a few days. The doctors who were sitting in the court knew the story well, they knew also about other riots of the red army men in the hospitals. The disturbance in the clinic of Sitkovsky of which Peters drew a picture in his speech did not surprise anyone. Just like Voyno-Yasenetsky, professor Sitkovsky simply could not physically cope with violent patients.

The second issue of the public prosecutor concerned the incident with "the worms." Voyno-Yasenetsky explained in detail to the court that there had been no worms under the bandages of the red army men at all, but larvae of flies. Surgeons are not afraid of such cases and do not hurry to clean wounds of larvae as it had long been observed that larvae are beneficial to the healing of wounds. English medics even used larvae as a sort of healing stimulants. Valentin Felixovich was an experienced lecturer so he explained the gist of the matter so clearly and convincingly, that the workers' part of the hall buzzed with approval.

"What larvae... How do you know all this?" Peters made himself angry.

"Let it be known to mister public prosecutor," said Voyno-Yasenetsky with dignity, "that I did not finish a two-year Soviet nursing school, but the medical faculty of the university of saint Vladimir in Kiev." The room applauded.

The last answer made the all-powerful Chekist lose his temper once and for all. His highest position of a government official demanded that the defiant expert was immediately exterminated, humiliated, crushed.
"Tell me, priest and professor Voyno-Yasenetsky, how can it be that you pray at night and cut people during the day?" continued Peters.
In fact, when the holy patriarch-confessor Tikhon learned that professor Voyno-Yasenetsky had taken holy orders he blessed him to continue doing surgery. Father Valentin did not explain anything to Peters, but replied:
"I cut people to save them, but in the name of what are you cutting people, mister public prosecutor?"
The hall met the apt response with laughter and applause. All sympathies were now on the side of the priest-surgeon. The workers and doctors applauded him. The next question Peters reckoned should change the mood of the workers' audience:
"How can it be that you believe in God, priest and professor Voyno-Yasenetsky? Did you see him, your God?"
"Indeed, I did not see God, mister public prosecutor, but I did a lot of brain operations and whenever I opened a skull I never saw a mind there either. And conscience I also did not find there." (The bell of the president drowned in the laughter of everyone in the hall. It did not grow silent for long.)
"The doctors' case" was an ignominious failure. However, to save the prestige of Peters, "the judges" sentenced professor Sitkovsky and his colleagues to sixteen years of imprisonment. This apparent injustice caused grumbling in the city. Then Chekists revoked the decision of "the trial" altogether. A month later the doctors were let out of their cell during the day to work in the hospital and two months later they were let out of jail completely. By all accounts the speech of priest-surgeon Voyno-Yasenetsky had saved them from execution.
Many weeks later it became known in the city that on the evening when the burnt red army men were brought in, professor Sitkovsky could not come to the clinic because his wife had tried to poison herself and he had to save her.
Five months after the trial of professor Sitkovsky yet another audit committee ordered to remove the icon in the operat-

ing room of the city hospital. Father Valentin announced he would not come to work until the icon was returned to its place. And he went home. At the end of 1921 such "sabotage" was punished as the heaviest political crime. Father Valentin was threatened with arrest. His friend M.I. Slonim wrote to the president of the Central Asian bureau of the central committee of the communist party, Rudzutaks, with a petition. He said that if the distinguished surgeon, scientist and pedagogue Voyno-Yasenetsky were arrested, the loss incurred by it would primarily be borne by the workers' and peasants' republic, its medicine and science. Rudzutaks graciously promised for the time being not to arrest the professor. Let the doctors themselves find a way out.

Father Valentin did not know anything about the petition by Slonim. He was on strike already for several days. Surgeons who were sent to him as "scouts" reported that the chief physician was working at his desk all the time, writing something, reading something. They tried to persuade him to no avail. According to the memoirs of professor Oshanin, a delegation of two or three doctors was sent to the archbishop of Turkestan. Vladyko promised to talk with father Valentin, and the next day Voyno-Yasenetsky went to work.

But the chief physician protested against the confiscation of the icon for a long time. He did not show up at the scientific medical society where he had to give a lecture. At the next meeting father Valentin was as always in a cassock. When he ascended the cathedra to give the lecture he first made the following statement: "I offer the society my apologies for the fact that I did not give the lecture on the day appointed for me. But it happened not because of a fault of mine. It happened through the fault of our healthcare commissar Gelfgot. A demon had got into him. He committed sacrilege over an icon." In the hall a deathly silence fell. Commissar Gelfgot attended the meeting. But he apparently was afraid of a scandal. The chairman of the scientific society professor M.A. Zakharchenko whispered to the secretary, doctor L.V. Oshanin, that he should not in any case record the disrespectful words about the public authority in the minutes of the meeting.

Even irreligious colleagues could not fail to notice the high morality of the orthodox priest, the future archbishop. In the 70's, former nurse at the Tashkent city hospital M.G.

Nezhanskaya said about him: "In cases requiring moral decisions, Valentin Felixovich behaved as if there was nobody around. He always stood before his conscience alone. And the court, by which he judged himself, was more severe than any tribunal." [P.]

41   Ps. 34:21 [tr.]

42   *Many of these studies on corpses were the basis of my book, "Essays on purulent surgery."*

"The extremely difficult path of a self-taught country surgeon that I had to go through taught me quite a lot which I would like to share now, towards the end of my work as a surgeon, with young comrades to ease their difficult tasks," wrote vladyko Luke in the preface to the first edition of his unique monograph, which became a desk book for doctors.

Physicians testify that the monograph of vladyko Luke is truly a classic, a fundamental work, covering virtually all aspects of purulent surgery. The material is set out in an unusually clear, precise, understandable way and at the same time highly professionally. Only a man who started his work by himself without practical help and guidance could write like that.

Before the era of antibiotics, when there was no other possibility to deal with purulence than through surgery, the book was simply indispensable. With the book a young specialist or a surgeon not specialized in purulence could perform complex operations in the difficult conditions of a country hospital. Many scholars noted that "Essays on purulent surgery" was written with great love for the suffering person and with great love for the reader.

"Published in 1934, 'Essays on purulent surgery' aroused universal interest. The distinguished surgeon I.I. Grekov gave an enthusiastic review of the book. Since then, for more than forty years, no significant work on purulent surgery appears without references to 'Essays on purulent surgery' and its author..." wrote V.I. Kolosov in 1977 ("Journal of Surgery," № 9). The first print of the book was instantly sold out. Requests for reprint were often made.

There are testimonies of non-Christians, that even not knowing that "Essays on purulent surgery" is written by bishop Luke, you cannot fail to notice that a Christian wrote the book. There are lines in it which reveal the Christian attention with which vladyko related to his patients: "When preparing the operation, it is necessary to bear in mind not only the abdominal cavity, but the whole diseased person, who unfortunately so often the doctors call 'a case'. The person is in his death throes and in fear of death, his heart trembles not only in a literal but also in a figurative sense. Therefore, not only carry out the very important task to reinforce the heart with camphor or digitalin, but also take care to save him from painful psychological traumas: the sight of the operating table, laid-out instruments, people in white lab coats, masks, rubber gloves. Anesthesize him outside the operating room. Take care of keeping him warm during surgery, because this is extremely important." [P.]

43   Lavrov.
44   Nomination is a stage before chirotony. [tr.]
45   Bessarion (born Vasily Zornin, 1878-1937). [tr.]
46   GPU. Governmental political directorate. Soviet secret police agency. Chronology of Soviet secret police agencies: Cheka 1917-1922, GPU 1922-1923, OGPU 1923-1934, NKVD-NKGB 1934-1943, NKGB-MGB 1943-1954, KGB 1954-1991. [tr.]
47   I do not remember his surname.
48   Prince Ukhtomsky.
49   Bishop Andrey (born prince Alexander Ukhtomsky) (1872-1944). In 1925 he deviated to the Old Believers' schism. Although he did not declare his adherence to the Old Believers, he was exposed and forbidden to serve by the locum tenens of the patriarchal throne, metropolitan of Krutitsy Peter. [P.]
50   The middle son of vladyko Luke Aleksey said: "One night, when I lay in my bed (in my father's study), Sofia Sergeyevna came in. Thinking that I was asleep, she began tearfully begging my father not to become a monk, for us, the children. But my father remained unbending." [P.]
51   His eminence Vasily (Zumer), bishop of Suzdal, vicar of Vladimir eparchy, died in the same year in exile in Uroteppa in Central Asia. [P.]
52   The Basmachi movement was an uprising against Russian imperial and Soviet rule by the Muslim, largely Turkic peoples of Central Asia. [tr.]
53   *With the bishops lived the exiled Moscow archpriest Sventsitsky...*

Archpriest Valentin Sventsitsky was born into a noble family in Kazan in 1882; in his youth he studied at Moscow university, he was a member of various philosophical circles, mostly with a religious inclination, he wrote short stories, novels, dramas, and he gave public lectures. In his younger years, and later V.P. Sventsitsky could remarkably affect people with his words in lectures and sermons, and in private conversations. He said that as a child he believed in God, but then there was a period, when he was sixteen-seventeen years old, when he came to a complete denial of God, and to despair. His state of mind was unbearable, he almost went mad. And then Valentin went to the Optina desert, the monastery famous for its startsi who led a life of sanctity. And he met starets Anatoly (Potapov). The starets had a profound effect on the young man, faith returned to him, deeper and more serious than it was before.

The events of 1905 allured V.P. Sventsitsky with ideas of Christian socialism and led him to organize the illegal society "Christian brotherhood of struggle," which also included P. Florensky, V. Ern, A. Elchaninov, father Jonah Brihnichev. Later Valentin Sventsitsky completely abandoned socialist ideas. In 1917 in Petrograd he was ordained a priest and then he moved to Moscow where he often served in different churches and preached. Soon father Valentin was sent to Panjakent in Central Asia.

When he came back in 1925 from his first exile, father Valentin Sventsitsky began to serve in the church of hieromartyr Pancras, where he regularly led discussions with parishioners about faith and church life. With the blessing of his holiness patriarch Tikhon he did six readings about the sacrament of penance, which were directed against collective confessions that were beginning to spread then. In these readings father Valentin argued, with many historical examples, that they were totally uncanonical and that such a practice is a distortion of the mystery (see "Hope," issue 2, Possev-Verlag, Frankfurt am Main, 1979).

The declaration of metropolitan Sergius (Stragorodsky) of 16th (29th) July 1927 caused father Valentin to protest sharply. He left for the Josephite schism. Father Valentin even forbade his spiritual children to attend churches that obeyed metropolitan Sergius. In 1928 father Valentin was arrested again and sent to Siberia. There, in a small village about eighty kilometers from the station Taishet he suffered a severe and agonizing illness. In exile father Valentin decided after much suffering to return to communion with metropolitan Sergius. In the face of death, he repented sincerely. Here are excerpts from a letter of Father Valentin to metropolitan Sergius:

Most eminent archbishop and all-merciful father, I am dying. Already for a long time my conscience troubles me, because I have sinned gravely before the holy orthodox church, and in the face of death this has become indubitable. I beg you to forgive my sin and reunite me with the holy orthodox church. I repent, that I conceived not to recognize you as the legitimate first bishop. It was out of pride and contrary to the holy canons. I rated my personal reasoning and personal sentiments higher than the conciliar reasoning of the church... I do not need anything, no freedom, no changes in external conditions, because now I'm waiting for my death, but for the sake of Christ, accept my repentance and let me die in unity with the holy orthodox church.

From letters to his spiritual children:

Your spiritual father made a terrible spiritual mistake and grievously sinned. Three years ago I separated from metropolitan Sergius and led my congregation from the bosom of the orthodox church. Woe to him through whom temptation comes into the world, and I have tempted many... I'm dying and in the face of death I acknowledge this was a terrible sin before the holy church and before you. Forgive me for Christ's sake and return with me to the bosom of the orthodox church, by repenting the separation, the falling away from orthodoxy, in which I have involved you. Those of you who will not lose faith in me as a spiritual leader, in spite of this terrible error of mine, let them stay with me in unity.

Human wisdom overshadowed the eternal and true wisdom. Councils foresaw all of history, they knew what horrors those sitting on the patriarchal thrones would do, they knew how much struggle, cruelty, and untruth there would be, how many unacceptable compromises verging on crime, and they knew what kind of temptation this would be for human souls, temptation similar to the one in which I drew you... they wisely guarded the human soul from these temptations by the strictest canons. The canons prescribe that only when the patriarch distorts the foundations of faith it is allowed not to recognize his authority... How it came about that this truth fully revealed itself to me is almost impossible to tell, but know that this is directly related to my near end. And maybe the Lord has saved me before my death and given me an opportunity to repent... It is terrible, it is beyond the strength of man, conscience. Such a terrible thing. It gives to bear such horrific burdens, but we cannot live without it.

Father Valentin Sventsitsky died on October 20th, 1931. He had received full forgiveness from metropolitan Sergius. The body of the deceased was allowed to be moved to Moscow. During the memorial services an endless stream of people walked by the grave. [P.]

54   Given the popularity of vladyko Luke (professor Voyno-Yasenetsky) amongst the people, the authorities feared something would happen, so his arrest was accompanied by a slander campaign in the "Workers' and peasants' press." They were followed by several libellous articles, clearly ordered by the GPU. And later in Soviet newspapers vladyko Luke was slandered repeatedly. Those attacking him in print included former archpriest Lomakin who had renounced God. [P.]

55   At the same time, vladyko Luke was accused of having connections with the British, which he made allegedly across the Turkish border. When talking about this, vladyko remarked with a smile: "I could not be a participant of the Cossack conspiracy or an international espionage agent for two reasons: firstly, that would run counter to my principles, and secondly, the security officials claimed that I operated in the Caucasus and the Ural simultaneously. All my attempts to explain that for one person that is physically impossible led to nothing." [P.]

56   Cheka. Emergency committee. Soviet secret police agency 1917-1922. [tr.]

57   According to the book of Popovski, it was Peters. [ed.] Yakov Khristoforovich Peters (1886-1938). [tr.]

58   Before vladyko Luke was sent in exile, he managed to appeal to the people's commissar of education A.V. Lunacharsky, who was also in charge of science and questions about publishing. The imprisoned professor asked the commissar not for freedom or a fair trial. He only wanted that on the cover of the future medical monograph next to the

author's surname his spiritual title would be indicated. Lunacharsky answered with a resolute refusal. The Soviet state publishing house cannot publish books of a "bishop Luke." Voyno-Yasenetsky was greatly disappointed. Later, in exile, he showed the typewritten response of the commissar to medical student F.I. Nakladov.

Subsequently, vladyko published in foreign journals some of his works in German. He signed them with "Bishop Luke." [P.]

59   The High Place is the name used for the location of the cathedra (episcopal throne), behind the altar. [tr.]

60   *...the Tashkent episcopal cathedra was already occupied by Living church metropolitan Nicholas. I called him "a ferocious wild boar who reclines on the High Place." I forbade people to associate with him. This last will of mine infuriated the Chekists.*

The full text of the will of vladyko Luke has survived. It was composed perhaps a few hours before his arrest:

It is my will that you will resolutely and unflinchingly observe to keep steadfastly to the path on which I have put you.

Submit to the administrative power if they confiscate your churches and if they give them to the wild boar. God has allowed him to be raised to the High Place of our cathedral. Don't get enticed by the exterior of the divine service, but also don't get tempted to blaspheme the worship done by the insubordinate boar. And if the boar seizes all churches, consider yourselves excommunicated by God from the churches and condemned to be starved of hearing the word of God. Don't have any communion with the boar and his acolytes and don't abase yourself by arguing with them.

Do not rise in rebellion against the authorities and humbly obey them. God has put them in power according to our sins. With the power of apostolic succession given to me by the Lord Jesus Christ, I command all the faithful of the Turkestan Church to strictly and unswervingly observe my will. Those who digress from it and go in prayerful communion with the boar I threaten with the wrath and judgment of God.

Your humble servant Luke

During an interrogation at the GPU, bishop Luke spoke about the Living church: "On behalf of Christ's church they sanctify and cover up all the works of the Soviet authorities whom they fawn upon. In so doing they violate the truth of Christ."

By mid-August, all the churches in the city had passed to the Living church. But... these churches were empty. "The will" of bishop Luke, a few dozen typewritten leaflets had a much greater impact on the parishioners than the condemnations in the newspapers by the party propagandists and the Living church people. In the GPU they understood: It was necessary to send vladyko Luke as soon as possible beyond the borders of Turkestan. [P.]

61   In the Resurrection church in the Kadashi suburb. [P.]

62   Metropolitan Arseny (Stadnitsky) died in exile in Tashkent in 1936. [P.]

63   Pyotr Arkadyevich Stolypin served as prime minister from 1906 to 1911. He was famous for encouraging millions of farmers to the eastern territories of Russia. They were transported in trains. Over the full length of the cars one side was designated for cattle and furniture. [tr.]

64   Purulent inflammation of bone tissue. [ed.]

65   A sequestrum is a piece of dead bone that has become separated during the process of necrosis fromsound bone. [tr.]

66   Congenital cataract is lens opacity present from birth. [tr.]

67   To this day in all the places of his exiles there are dozens of people who remember bishop Luke with gratitude. Vladyko Luke did not refuse to help especially the most forlorn and poverty-stricken. He did not take anything for treatment. He could spend days bothering with sickly and dirty village children.

For each operation at which bishop Luke collaborated he was supposed to get a separate permit that was given grudgingly, and the growing popularity of the exiled annoyed the heads of the city. In Yeniseysk people tell that he was once called to the political directorate. As soon as he, as always in a cassock and with a cross, stepped into the office, the Chekist shouted: "Who gave you the permission to practice?" Vladyko Luke said, "I do not practice in the sense you give to that word. I do not take money from patients. And I don't have the right to refuse patients, I am really sorry."

They repeatedly sent "scouts" to vladyko-doctor and it was proven that he did not take payment from patients at all. In response to the gratitude of patients he answered: "It was God who healed you with my hands. Pray to Him." After that, the authorities began to look at the medical practice of the exiled professor more leniently. At the time along the Yenisei river trachoma was raging. Because of this disease many local inhabitants - Kets, Selkups, Evenks - lost their eyesight. The former head of the Yenisei shipping company I.M. Nazarov shares some words of Evenk driver Nikita from lower Imbatska he heard in the thirties: "A great shaman with a white beard came to our river, a priest-shaman. When the priest-shaman speaks a word, a blind person immediately becomes able to see. Then the priest-shaman left and the eyes of everybody are diseased again." Captain Nazarov believes that this talk was about the exiled professor Voyno-Yasenetsky, who operated patients from the effects of trachoma very well. [P.]

68   In Yeniseysk the outrages of the Komsomol atheists against religion were on a particularly big scale. A former policeman told with great willingness how he himself at that time ripped off gold mountings from icons of the Dormition cathedral, how he loaded on a cart requisitioned chalices and incense burners, how he helped to drag the bells down from the church. During the requisitions believers - sometimes several hundreds of people - would gather standing at a distance, railing at the authorities and the Komsomol activists. Damnations and prayers to punish the blasphemers were heard. A policeman fired a warning shot into the air, some were taken to the police station. In the winter of 1924 the Komsomol ruined the chapel in the village of Sotnikovo, "just for a laugh." A former scout leader recalls that during the entire year of 1924 in Yeniseysk there were thundering explosions: The Komsomol members were destroying the churches, led by their secretary, who also organized blasphemous carnivals and performances.

Vladyko Luke preached several sermons denouncing this impiety. He put the destroyers of churches to shame and took part in a crowded public debate with the young medic-atheist Chegletsov. With this, vladyko Luke antagonized the Yeniseysk party authorities and Soviet authorities even more.

Also some local doctors were hostile to bishop Luke. Or rather, it was the former doctor's assistants, who were hostile. At that time they ran private practices as an alternative to experienced doctors. But Voyno-Yasenetsky deprived them of their clientele. These entrepreneurs of medicine, who made a fortune in the New Economic Policy years, hypocritically complained to the authorities about "a priest" who carries out "irresponsible" operations... [P.]

69 Komsomol. All-Union Leninist young communist league was the youth division of the communist party of the Soviet Union. [tr.]

70 Chaya is a village of eight houses surrounded by an endless forest wilderness. In March, it is still deep winter there. The houses are often covered with snow up to the roof. In the morning he had to wait until a path was made, so as to be able to bring in brushwood to kindle the stove. In the inner porch the water in the water dispenser froze.

With deep Christian patience vladyko Luke endured all the hardships of the exile: "Do not worry about me, I do not need anything," he wrote to his son Mikhail from Yeniseysk, and a few months later: "Do not worry about me. The Lord accommodated me excellently in Chaya. I'm joyful, deeply calm, I do not feel any needs, the nuns are taking care of me with great love." [P.]

71 Tapeworm. [tr.]

72 Trachoma is a chronic viral eye disease. If not treated it leads to corneal ulceration, the eyelids folding inwards, the formation of cataracts, blindness. [ed.]

73 According to the words of one ordinary elderly woman who was a nurse's aid in the district hospital "all people" in Turukhansk still know "professor Luke." She remembers with gratitude how he restored health to a great number of people, despite the fact that the equipment in the hospital in the twenties was most primitive: the instruments, for example, were boiled in a samovar before an operation...

They say that vladyko Luke was badly off and almost did not have anything, only books. [P.]

74 *The Turukhansk monastery was closed. However, an old priest performed all church services there.*

The name of the priest was father Martin Rimsha. Prior to belonging the ecclesiastical rank he had been a teacher for almost forty years in villages in his native Belarus. He was a deeply religious man, an intellectual. Because of his heart disease he had left teaching. In Moscow he had completed pastoral courses for Siberia from archpriest Ioan Vostorgov (†1917) and together with his whole large family he went to Yenisei shortly before the first world war. The Turukhansk farmers respected father Martin. Often bolsheviks who had been exiled to Turukhansk came to him to talk.

After hearing from vladyko Luke with what kind of political leaven the Living church was kneaded, father Martin understood and easily turned away from the schism. In the life of father Martin there was great grief. He had done his best to bring up his daughter with faith and piety: he had sent her to the eparchial college, and then to continue learning to the Yeniseysk monastery. Vera had good abilities. Sacred history and catechism came easily to her. But the girl completely lost faith in God, perhaps because of studying Christianity more in the letter than in the spirit. And - as used to happen at the beginning of the revolution - she became an activist, left her parents, went to Krasnoyarsk, got married, and became a Komsomol atheist.

After the death of her mother, Vera came to visit her father and brothers. She brought several issues of the magazine "The godless" with her. At that time that magazine published "The Bible for unbelievers" of Yemelyan Yaroslavsky. Vera's father called these writings "satanic philosophy."

[Yemelyan Yaroslavsky (Gubelman Minei Izrailevich), party figure, led the "league of militant atheists" (SVB), founded in 1925, based on the group of activists of the newspaper "Atheist." This pogrom organization caused irreparable damage to the country's culture. The league could take advantage of a monopoly in the field of ideology, because it had an extensive network of periodicals (the newspaper "Atheist," the magazines "The godless," "Atheist," "The antireligious," "The young godless," and others). With its own publishing house, the league de facto launched a broad campaign of slander, blasphemy and vilification of the holy church. It inspired both ordinary "godless people" and the fooled "popular masses" to pogroms. Desecration, closing and destruction of churches, burning of icons, ubiquitous and almost daily insults of orthodox people - this is not a complete list of the evil deeds of the league of militant atheists. Krupskaya, Krasikov, Skvortsov-Stepanov, Demyan Bedny and others collaborated with the league. During the war the league virtually stopped

its ignominious existence. In 1947, its functions were transferred to the national society for the dissemination of political and scientific knowledge (society "Knowledge"). (ed.)]
Soon after this vladyko Luke appeared in Turukhansk. Vera Martinovna Savinskaya herself recalled:
One of the first of his questions to my father was: "To whom do you obey, father, to the renovators or the Tikhonites?"
"Both write to me so I have to answer both."
"Patriarch Tikhon has the right faith, and the revivalists crawl for the Soviet authorities," said the bishop.
At that time the daughter of father Martin did not like it that her father was under the influence of the exiled Tikhonite. But it was even more annoying for her that vladyko Luke, in her words, "without knowing it brought to naught all of her anti-religious propaganda." "Prior to his arrival," writes Savinskaya, "just a few people went to church, but with his arrival the influx of parishioners in the church significantly increased. People from Turukhansk told me that on the twelve major holidays believers covered the road from the hospital to the church for him with red cloth, carpets and rugs. And my father even stopped answering my letters..."
Many years later, Vera Martinovna regretted that she did not want to meet bishop Luke in 1926. He had returned from exile and was in Krasnoyarsk. He sent her an invitation to visit. Father Martin was subsequently arrested for disobeying the authorities. His disobedience had been expressed by his refusal to be present at the opening of the relics of holy martyr Vasily Mangazeysky that were resting in the former convent in Turukhansk. Father Martin endured twelve years of exiles and camps. In 1936 he wrote to his daughter that he would like to come to Krasnoyarsk. By that time she thought her father long dead. "When we met," remembers Vera Martinovna, "my father showed me a whole stack of mail receipts. Vladyko Luke, it turns out, had been making monthly transfers of 30 rubles all the while, and more often of fifty rubles." Father Martin Rimsha died in 1941, in his daughter's house. [P.]
75   As in Tashkent vladyko Luke had an icon with a lighted lamp in front of it on a small table in the operating room. They say that before an operation vladyko made a cross on the body of the patient with iodine. [P.]

76   This deportation was tantamount to premeditated murder. In the dead of winter, which was particularly brutal this year, to send a person on an open sleigh half a thousand versts away with no warm clothes, meant to condemn him to inevitable death. The chairman of the provincial council of Turukhansk (a red partisan, hero of the civil war F.I. Babkin) as a native inhabitant of Yenisei understood this very well. [P.]

77   Socialist revolutionary Rosenfeld was a Jew from Belarus and fundamentally an atheist and materialist. On this basis more than once there had been heated bouts with the bishop. But as soon as Rosenfeld learned of the exile of Voyno-Yasenetsky, he undertook to go to the homes of his fellow socialist revolutionaries and in the end he gathered a whole bunch of warm water breams and even a little money. [P.]

78   Kureika 1914-1917. [tr.]

79   Malyuta Skuratov was one of the most odious leaders during the reign of Ivan the Terrible. Saint Philip II of Moscow was a Russian Orthodox monk, who became metropolitan of Moscow during the reign of Ivan the Terrible. He was one of the few metropolitans who dared openly to contradict the royal authority, and it is widely believed that the tsar had him murdered on that account. [tr.]

80   A sazhen is a measure of length (two thousand hundred and thirty four metres).

81   A sweet drink resembling thin jelly.

82   The book of needs is a liturgical book containing sacramental rites performed by the church in special cases that are not part of the daily, weekly or annual cycle of public church services. [tr.]

83   *In Plakhino I spent a little more than two months...*
Once in Plakhino bishop Luke was visited by A.K. Konstantinov. He was a former postal and trade official, and in the twenties he was the commissioner of the Moscow bureau of fur harvesting. The head of the Turukhansk post office, whose sick child vladyko Luke had saved, had given correspondence to Konstantinov to pass on to the exiled bishop. With this Konstantinov violated a strict prohibition of the authorities. When Konstantinov crossed the snow-covered threshold he looked into a sooty hut that had not been swept for a long

time. There was also an unbleached oven and armfuls of firewood lying near it. The squalour and poverty of the dwelling was discernible in everything. On an unpainted table stood a glass of water and lay a piece of black bread. He didn't see any other food. Bishop Luke was praying. With a gesture he asked the guest to wait a bit. Ten minutes later, after having made a final bow before the large age-old icon, he turned to his guest and said: "And now we will get acquainted."

After learning that the women refused to cook for vladyko Luke and that there was in general nothing to cook, Konstantinov wrote a message to the two nearest trading posts so that henceforth they would sell the professor wheat flour, sugar, pretzels, and durum wheat. It turned out that vladyko Luke had no money and the guest offered to lend him a hundred rubles. After that, on the road, at the request of the bishop, Konstantinov managed to send a telegram to his family, even though in those years personal telegrams were not accepted. When he was talking with Konstantinov, vladyko Luke told him about his possible return to Turukhansk (the well-known Siberian surgeon professor V.M. Myt was taking trouble about this), and added: "The Lord God has given me to know that in a month I'll be in Turukhansk." Konstantinov gave him a perplexed look, and vladyko shook his head and said: "I see, I see, you are not a believer. For you my words seem incredible, but it will be that way." After a week and a half Konstantinov visited Plakhino for a second time but by that time it turned out that vladyko Luke already was no longer there: the exiled had been taken to Turukhansk. [P.]

84   *This second stay of mine in Turukhansk lasted for eight months...*

At that time vladyko Luke wrote to the academic Pavlov, the famous physiologist, a deeply religious man:

Beloved brother of mine in Christ and highly esteemed colleague, Ivan Petrovich!

Banished because of Christ to the world's end (for three months I lived at four hundred versts north of Turukhansk), I was almost completely cut off from the world, so I only just found out about the celebration in your honour on the occasion of the seventy fifth anniversary of your glorious life and the upcoming celebration of the two hundredth anniversary of the science academy. Please accept my belated greeting. I praise God Who has given you such great strength of mind and has blessed your labours. I deeply bow before you for your great work. And apart from my deep respect, accept my love and my blessing because of your piety, rumour of which has reached me from those knowing you.

I regret that my greeting cannot be in time for the academic celebration.

May the grace and mercy of our Lord Jesus Christ be with you. Humble Luke, bishop of Tashkent and Turkestan (former professor of topographic anatomy and operative surgery Voyno-Yasenetsky)

Turukhansk, 28.08.1925

This letter was written on a little sheet torn out of a notebook, on top is put a cross. In response to these congratulations I.P. Pavlov wrote to bishop Luke in Turukhansk:

Your eminence and dear comrade!

I am deeply moved by your warm greeting and offer my heartfelt thanks for it. In a difficult time, full of persistent grief for those who are thinking and feeling, feeling humanely, there remains one vital foothold: to fulfill as much as one can the duty one has assumed. I sympathize with you with all my heart in your martyrdom.

Yours truly and faithfully,

Ivan Pavlov [P.]

85   Ps. 31:8-9.
86   Iridectomy is the surgical removal of part of the iris. [ed.]
87   A light, open, four-wheeled horse-drawn carriage. [tr.]
88   *[In Tashkent] I was only occupied with receiving patients at my home, so of course I did not cease to pray... at all services...*

Vladyko Luke lived not far from the Sergius church. On the day assigned to make appointments with patients, people would gather under the windows the night before. At five in the morning signing up started and after one and a half to two hours more than four hundred surnames were accumulated on the list for the next month.

X.F. Pankrateva, a pensioner from Tashkent, recalls the following incident: When she was sixteen years old she was told at the clinic that she was ill with pulmonary tuberculosis. This led her into turmoil. Good people advised her to go to the bishop-professor. The girl hesitated for a long time to make an appointment with such a famous person. Raised in a family of non-believers, she had no cross. Xenia made an appointment, but her turn came only after a month. The friendly doctor carefully examined and listened to the little girl-patient. He said that her lungs really were weak, but far from tuberculosis. He recommended a strict diet and advised her to go to a kumis [mare-milk (tr.)] health resort. He asked: "Do you have money for such a trip?" Xenia had never heard that vladyko Luke not only healed, but also provided financial assistance to poor patients. The girl hurried to say that she had money for the treatment and the trip, and vladyko let her out after having blessed her for the road.

Once vladyko Luke noticed on the steps of the city hospital a teenage girl and a small boy. Sensitive to other people's troubles, he immediately suspected something was wrong and went to the children. It turned out that their father had died, and the only close person in the city, their mother, was in the hospital, and apparently for long. Luke took the children into his house and hired a woman look after them until their mother recovered.

The girl (her name was Shura Kozhushko), who was fifteen-sixteen years old then, began to help vladyko Luke at the medical visiting hours. She quickly mastered the basics of medicine and after a year, without having gone through any educational institution, she had become a good nurse. Vladyko Luke would invariably send Shura around the city to look for sick people in need of help or material support. One of the patients she found was the orphan Raya Purtova.

This girl came to Tashkent immediately after secondary school in the hope of continuing her studies. Unfortunately she contracted pneumonia, lay alone in a strange house, and there was no one to treat and care for her. Raya was exhausted. At that time antibiotics were not used yet, she could well have died. At the request of bishop Luke in a devout family, they began to give proper food to the girl. Raya gained strength, got to her feet. Several times she came to the doctor who saved her as a patient, and then she became friends with Shura Kozhushko and became "one of us" in the house. On the instructions of vladyko Luke, she gladly searched for people just like herself, poor people who had been ailing for long. Those whom Shura and she found, vladyko Luke would visit himself later and he would help with money. For a long time the house on Uchitelskaya street was for Raya her most dear place.

After finishing work, the girls would come to the office of vladyko Luke that was crammed with bookshelves. The bishop sat in an armchair, the girls on benches next to him. They talked about different life situations and books they had read. Raya remembered these words vladyko Luke once said: "The main thing in life is always to do good to people. If you cannot do big good things for people, try to do at least little good things."

"Any conversation would somehow take such a turn that we would begin to understand the value of a person, the importance of an ethical life," recalls Raisa Petrovna afterwards. "Why do you come to me?" vladyko once asked Raya. "Obviously you come to me for affection? In your life there was probably little affection..."

Uzbeks living in Tashkent highly respected the bishop-doctor. A multitude of sick Uzbeks came to the house on Uchitelskaya street. Shura acted as translator, because she was fluent in Uzbek. All honoured vladyko Luke, they turned to him also for the resolution of family and domestic conflicts.

After the Liturgy, when leaving the church, bishop Luke was usually accompanied by a large crowd. The people's love for vladyko especially flowed on his name day, October 31st. In the church the worship was conducted solemnly. The crowds of believers did not fit under the arches of the saint Sergius church. They filled the church yard and even part of Pushkin street. From the house of the bishop to the church for two blocks the road was strewed with late autumn flowers. And in the yard of the house where the Voyno-Yasenetsky's lived, from the porch to the gates, there were white chrysanthemums in pots. [P.]

89   *On April 23rd, 1930, I was arrested a second time.*

City officials wanted to get rid of vladyko Luke - retired bishop, professor deprived of a student audience, scientist whose books were not printed. They wanted to drive one more undefeated Christian out of the city. In 1929 they began to look for an excuse to exile vladyko Luke. The GPU did not need real violations of state laws, and soon a pretext for the arrest of the influential bishop presented itself. Using it they could also get some political gain. They fabricated an absurd accusation of the bishop.

Professor physiologist I.P. Mikhaylovsky became ill with violent insanity when he lost his son in 1924. He begged to be killed. Although he had previously been a religious man, he came to mad grumbling against God and blasphemy, he hacked icons to pieces with an ax. He refused to bury his son, said he would resurrect him, and he began experiments with blood transfusion. The professor soaked the boy's body in formalin and placed it in a closet at the sub-faculty, wrapped in a reed mat. He bought clothes, shoes and sweets for the dead boy. Mikhaylovsky became rude and cruel, it happened that he beat his wife and children. Then his spouse left him. Five years later he married a twenty year old girl and married her in the church. Soon the unfortunate professor shot himself.

The same day, his young widow came to bishop Luke, told him about the suicide and tearfully asked vladyko to plead for Mikhaylovsky so that a funeral service would be held for him, and he would be buried according to church custom. Vladyko Luke was not the ruling bishop, so that was also why he could not give permission for such a funeral. But he felt sorry for the poor woman and he wrote a note to metropolitan Arseny. Vladyko Arseny answered: "According to the old laws a medical certificate was required attesting the psychological insanity of the one who shot himself. In that case a church burial is possible." Bishop Luke wrote on a small sheet of paper with his name stamp:

I certify that I personally know professor Mikhaylovsky. He took his own life in a state of undoubted mental illness from which he suffered for more than two years.

MD bishop Luke, 05.08.1929

The soviet investigator who led the case of Mikhaylovsky preferred for political reasons, to make it a case not of suicide, but of murder, and the widow of the professor was accused. In the press appeared stories of this tragedy. The religiosity of Mikhaylovsky's second wife was indicated as the motive of the murder. He, allegedly, had been an ardent atheist, and unequivocal political allusions were made. Also in Moscow they became interested in the case; it had been submitted for further investigation and at the GPU they decided to turn it into a political and anti-religious matter. And vladyko Luke was drawn in too. The certificate given by him was used as the principal document used for the prosecution.

From his cell bishop Luke sent a note to the investigator: "For your information, I do not believe the seriousness of the charges against me in the case of Mikhaylovsky at all. The reason for my arrest, of course, is my answer to prosecutor G. (Goldovsky) during his last visit to me..." An answer followed neither to this, nor to another note. The investigator of the GPU called the major medics of the city one by one to his office. He wanted to get "scientifically founded" evidence of the conflict between Voyno-Yasenetsky with the "materialist" Mikhaylovsky. But the scientists persistently talked about Mikhaylovsky's mental unsoundness, and about bishop Luke they gave very respectful, even deferential opinions. There had been no conflict at all and there could not have been any. Some assistant-dissector at professor Mikhaylovsky's sub-faculty gave the necessary evidence. He was an uneducated village chap but also a party activist. He was involved in the case by an ingenious new investigator. The evidence, in part, was as follows: "The experiments of professor I.P. Mikhaylovsky dramatically shake religious foundations. The professor's wife is religious. The certificate about the 'mental disorder' of professor Mikhaylovsky issued by professor-medic Yasenetsky (Luke) is deliberately false. It can be interpreted first of all as a document which had the purpose of hiding a criminal offense, the murder of Mikhaylovsky. It puts in the foreground suicide on the basis of a mental disorder he had for the past two years. But it is a murder to eliminate Mikhaylovsky, with the purpose of protecting religious foundations of thought... etc."

Professors Slonim and Ragoza gave investigator Pleshanov an official certificate stating that V.F. Voyno-Yasenetsky suffers from aortic sclerosis, cardiosclerosis and significant heart dilation. The top therapists of Tashkent wrote that "because of the nature of his disease Voyno-Yasenetsky requires strict rest and prolonged systematic treatment." The same was written by MD V.A. Sokolov, who treated vladyko for decompensation of the heart. To the statements of the doctors, no one paid any attention. The daughter of the defendant, Elena Valentinovna, sought permission to see her father to give him the necessary heart medicine. A resolution followed: "Don't comply." Bishop Luke asked the investigator to allow him to receive scientific books. The application was marked: "Refused." In the overcrowded cell with no air to breathe vladyko Luke lost consciousness after an interrogation. The prison administration pretended that nothing had happened.

A few days after he had fainted vladyko Luke was lifted from the bed and led to the office of investigator Pleshanov. They read him again the indictment that had been drawn up:

City of Tashkent, July 6th, 1930

... And taking into account 1) that Voyno-Yasenetsky... is proven guilty of giving on 5th August 1929, i.e. the day of Mikhaylovsky's death, a deliberately false certificate of the mentally abnormal state of health of Mikhaylovsky with the purpose of dulling the attention of forensic examination, because he wanted to cover up the traces of the crime of the de facto murder of Mikhaylovsky by his wife Ekaterina, 2) that this is accordingly established by testimonies of the accused and by documents that pertain to the case, 3) that these criminal deeds are provided for in articles 10-14 and 186 point 1 of the criminal code of the Uzbek SSR

... DECREED

To draw in citizen Voyno-Yasenetsky Valentin Felixovich as an accused, and charge him with concealment of murder according to articles 10-14 and 186 point 1 of the criminal code of the Uzbek SSR.

signed, Pleshanov, commissioner

approved, Butenko, head of the secret department

confirmed, Karutsky, secret-operative administration

Vladyko Luke listened to all this nonsense standing . Sweat was pouring off him, his hands wer shaking from weakness, his knees were bent a little, but he found the strength in himself to dip the pen in ink and write under the printed text: "The accusation was brought against me on June 13th, 1930. I plead not guilty." A few hours later, bishop Luke was already in the prison hospital. His heart irrevocably became much worse.

Vladyko Luke spent a year in prison cells, deprived of books, parcels from outside, visits of family and friends. The investigation was completed, but at the GPU they were still negotiating about something. In winter it became damp and cold in the suffocating prison cells. Archbishop Luke was ill. He was taken to the hospital several times, then back again for questioning. Then, from the internal prison of the GPU he was transferred to the general prison. Only on May 15th of the next year, 1931, came the record of the proceedings at a special meeting of the collegium of the GPU. Three unknown persons decided in absence: "...Valentin Felixovich Voyno-Yasenetsky is to be sent through the GPU commissioner to the Northern province for a period of three years as from May 6th 1930." Ekaterina Mikhaylovskaya forfeited the right to live on twelve locations and was sent to the Chita or Omsk district for three years.

Vladyko Luke wrote three times to the investigator and his superiors and he asked to replace exile to Siberia with exile to Central Asia or Chinese Turkestan, but he was refused.

In the "Workers' and peasants' press" the case of Mikhaylovsky received unprecedented coverage. By "social order" a series of works of art were written: a novel by Borisoglebsky: "On the verge," a play by Trenev: "Experience," a drama by B. Lavrenev: "We will live!" In each of them a brilliant scientist-materialist, who comes close to discover how to bring the dead to life, becomes a "victim of religious fanaticism." There were even scientists who made statements in the press that these writings were utterly unscientific. [P.]

90   Parishioner of the Dormition cathedral in Tashkent A.A. Medyntseva recalls:

Vladyko Luke always said that no one should condemn anyone. When the service was over, he said: "Brothers and sisters, today I have not prayed for *you*, but I prayed for the brethren who have sinned. But to all of you I say: do not condemn the clergy. It is better to condemn the whole world, than one spiritual person." That night he was arrested...

The mother of Anna Alexandrovna told her how they transferred vladyko Luke: "A few people gathered , then we went and watched from a distance: as if he were a hooligan, they tugged at his beard, spat in his face. Somehow I could not help remembering that Jesus Christ was mocked just as he was." [P.]

91   Kulaks. peasants in Russia wealthy enough to own a farm and hire labour. They resisted forced collectivization. Millions were arrested, exiled, or killed. [tr.]
92   At this time in Archangelsk all the churches were closed. At the hospital where bishop Luke worked, the room for outpatients was small, very cramped, half dark. The queue was always crowded together in the corridor, women were cursing, children were crying. The stoves were smoking, but gave little heat. There was a shortage of cotton wool, bandages, antiseptics, even paper. Prescriptions were written on scraps of paper, and patient histories on newspaper, in purple ink across the printed text. There were always many patients: forty or more signed up every day for the surgeon. This second exile vladyko Luke considered easy. [P.]
93   Nikolai Nikolayevich Petrov (1876-1964). [tr.]
94   Jn. 21:16. [ed.]
95   Jules Gonin (1870-1935) was a professor of ophthalmology in Lausanne. [tr.]
96   Viktor Petrovich Odintsov (1876-1938). [tr.]
97   *On discharge from the hospital I returned to Tashkent...*
After the second operation on vladyko Luke's diseased eye, he learned that his son Mikhail had had an accident: the train on which he was travelling from Leningrad to Moscow had crashed. Mikhail Voyno-Yasenetsky was wounded in several places. His wounds included a severe leg fracture. He was taken to a hospital in Leningrad. Bishop Luke hastened to Leningrad hoping to help his son. But he left before completing treatment and as a result his undertreated eye was lost once and for all.
In Tashkent in 1935, bishop Luke lived near Poltoratsky hospital. Early in the morning a car would drive up to his house. He was driven to the church, and the car was waiting for him at the church fence till the end of the service. Then vladyko Luke went to the institute of emergency aid, the third building of which he directed. Thus began a day filled with operations, consultations, conferences. After working in the operating theatre and on the corpses he read lectures at the institute of advanced training of doctors specialization. On Saturdays, Sundays and holidays they sent a horse-drawn carriage from the church for vladyko Luke.

Many doctors gladly studied with bishop Luke. The professor insisted that the doctors always did everything possible to save a patient. He said that they have no right to even think about failure. The bishop-surgeon was always filled with indignation by cases of lack of professionalism and ignorance in medical work, from which people suffered and which in Soviet medicine were unfortunately not uncommon. Vladyko Luke did not tolerate indifference to medical duty.

Once bishop Luke had to fly to Stalinabad to urgently operate on a prominent party member who was dying. After that the Stalinabad officials offered the exiled bishop to stay and work with them, but he agreed to come only in the event the city would build a church. The authorities did not go along with that.

In the healthcare commissariat and the surgical society they knew that vladyko Luke treated Tashkent and Stalinabad officials, and in spite of the fact that they repeatedly slandered the exiled bishop, he was not arrested then. In the same year they wrote in "Truth of the east" that "the people's healthcare commissariat of Uzbekistan approved the degree of doctor of medicine of professor V.F. Voyno-Yasenetsky without a thesis. The healthcare commissariat took into account the twenty seven years of work of Voyno-Yasenetsky and his achievements in the field of purulent surgery. His dissertation, which he defended in 1916, has not lost its importance..." In fact, the surgeon's medical work had continued for over thirty three years. For some reason the healthcare commissariat did not include six years exile and prison... [P.]

98   Phil. 2:17. "Yea, and if I be offered upon the sacrifice and service of your faith, I joy, and rejoice with you all."

99   Flm. 1:7.

100   On the eve of his arrest vladyko Luke's house was searched. It happened, as usual, at night. Several people in civilian clothes, a policeman and the yardman came in. They removed icons, rummaged in drawers and cabinets. A young Chekist shuffled through a box of letters from the late Anna Lanskaya. Vladyko Luke sat in the corner without saying a word. Onto a pile in the middle of the room flew books, clothing, medical manuscripts. The young Chekist asked permission to smoke. The bishop replied, "You dig in the letters of

my wife, you do I don't know what in my house, so continue doing what you want..."
At this time vladyko Luke was sixty years old, and his left eye was completely blind. [P.]

101   *[In the central provincial jail] I spent about eight months in very difficult conditions.*
Muhammad Omarovich Rahim, the cousin of the Afghan emir, testified about the stay of vladyko Luke there. He was a Muslim, who had fled to Soviet territory during the revolt in Kabul, where he was arrested on charges of espionage. In 1938, he was detained in the provincial prison in the seventh cell of the second building, together with vladyko Luke.
Muhammad Rahim speaks with respect about the orthodox bishop. According to his memoirs, in the cell there were sitting together "white" and "red" generals, secretaries of provincial committees, members of the central committee, professors, cadets, anarchists, communists and non-party people. Often there occurred disputes, mutual recriminations were voiced. The most ardent atheists tried to draw into the dispute the "irresponsible and reactionary" bishop, but vladyko refused to argue about faith. In his medical lectures (other professors also gave such lectures) he did not touch political issues. In the cell he was even-tempered and reserved with everybody, he was ready to provide anyone with medical help, he would share his bread ration as well. The people in the cell related to vladyko Luke in general respectfully. Even the authorities singled him out: vladyko was freed from cleaning toilets and taking out the close-stool. "He was the kind of person you wouldn't treat otherwise," explains Muhammad Rahim.
Bishop Luke told him a lot about his past. There was a story that stuck in his memory of how in Siberia he had to do an abdominal operation on a peasant with a penknife, and sew up the wound with women's hair, and there was no suppuration at that.
Muhammad Rahim said that from the prison bishop Luke wrote to defense commissar K.E. Voroshilov about his book, that it was indispensable in our country in peace time, but even more in the event of war. He did not ask to be freed, but he just wanted to get scientific material from his house, and at least for two hours a day, withdraw to work...

Vladyko Luke openly practiced his faith. He also did not conceal the fact that he was prosecuted for it. He said: "They repeat to me over and over again to take off my cassock, but I will never do that. It will stay with me until my death." And he said as well: "I do not know what they want from me. I'm a believer. I help people as a doctor, and I help as a minister of the church. For whom is this bad? The GPU employees attack me like kites. What for?"

In the cell where bishop Luke lived it became the custom that some of the prisoners, before they went in for questioning, came up to the bishop for a blessing. This was reported, and vladyko was called to the prison hospital, where doctor Oboyev tried to persuade him for a long time to take off his cassock and generally "not to attract too much attention." Afterwards Oboyev acknowledged to an acquaintance of his that he had not succeeded to carry out this order of the head of the prison. Bishop Luke correctly, but firmly, told his colleague that he had taken up a mission beyond his strength.

Professor of dermatology from Tashkent A.A. Akovbyan had at some time attended lectures by professor Voyno-Yasenetsky at the university. Later, when he found himself in the same cell with vladyko, he noted that the grief experienced by bishop Luke had not crushed him in the least, but on the contrary, it had strengthened and tempered his soul. Vladyko kneeled twice a day, turned to the east, and prayed, not noticing anything around him. In the cell, filled to capacity with tortured, embittered people, it would suddenly become quiet. All the people around him, and among them were Muslims as well as non-believers, would begin to whisper, and somehow the quarrels that just before had been tearing the people apart resolved themselves.

During the distribution of the morning rations, when the atmosphere in the cell was strained to the limit, vladyko Luke used to sit aside, and in the end there was always someone who would hand him a chunk of bread no worse than those that others got, and sometimes even the crust. Later, in early 1939, at the end of the Yezhov terror, it was allowed to receive parcels. According to Armais Aristagesovich, when vladyko received parcels, he gave away everything until the last crumb to the other prisoners.

Vladyko Luke never complained and never spoke about the accusations that were brought against him. He also did not complain after the thirteen day round-the-clock interrogation conveyor. They say that no one endured more than thirteen days. After the "conveyor" vladyko was dragged into the cell. According to bishop Luke's daughter, Elena Valentinovna Zhukova-Voyno, during one of these interrogations a Chekist burst into the investigation room several times, colourfully dressed as a clown. He spewed ugly curses and insults, mocked the faith, and predicted a terrible end for the bishop. Only just before he walked out to go on transport, according to the memoirs of A.A. Akovbyan, vladyko turned for the first time to the Tashkent doctors and scientists who were imprisoned with him. He asked: "Whom God will allow to be freed prison, let him petition together with other professors to ease my fate. After all, I did not do anything wrong. Maybe the government will listen to your requests..." Six months later, in the summer of 1940, Armais Aristagesovich passed this request on to professor M.I. Slonim. But the old friend of vladyko Luke, now already decorated, a deputy, an honoured doctor, frightfully waved his hands: "What, what, no, no..."

Elena Valentinovna narrates that for almost two years after the arrest of vladyko Luke, his children did not know anything about him. The first pieces of news leaked from the prison hospital: Dad lies with oedema of the legs, and due to his hunger strikes his heart is weakened. Afterwards the family was allowed to bring parcels. In the summer of 1939 Elena Valentinovna stood at the iron gates of the prison yard. During the time of the prisoners' airing she twice saw her father through a hole made by pushing a nail through the fence. An acquainted Persian prisoner who was carrying a pan with gruel shouted loudly, "Make way! Make way!" And on passing near Elena he whispered: "He is healthy, healthy." Then she learned that vladyko Luke had declared he was going on hunger strike and he was taken to the hospital. Once she received a note from her father: "In twenty four hours I'll be home." Neither in a day, nor in a week did he come home. The next note, passed on by a hospital orderly reported: "I was deceived, they will not release me, I resumed my hunger strike." He was fasting at that time for eighteen days. [P.]

102 *In Krasnoyarsk they kept us, not for long, in some forwarding prison on the outskirts of the city and from there they brought us to the village of Bolshaya Murtha...*

Before the war there were in the district center Bolshaya Murtha on the Yenisei tract three and a half thousand people. In the book of incoming patients vladyko Luke registered them as "farmers."

The chief doctor of the district hospital A.V. Barsky, who was at that time twenty-six years old, remembers how late one evening in early March bishop Luke came to his hospital:

In came a tall old man with a broad and thick white beard and he introduced himself: "I am professor Voyno-Yasenetsky." This surname was known to me only from the book "Essays on purulent surgery." He told me that he had just arrived in a very large group of ex-prisoners from Krasnoyarsk on carts. They were victims of 1937. They had been sent to the Bolshaya Murtha district to settle freely... As a surgeon he had decided to apply first of all to the district hospital and he asked me to provide him with only linen and food, and he promised to help me with surgical work. I was a bit stunned but delighted with such help and such a meeting.

Doctor Barsky said that during their collaboration, he received from professor Voyno-Yasenetsky essentially a practical course of surgery. With great difficulty he managed to get permission for the exiled bishop-professor to work in the hospital.

"... The head of district healthcare," says Barsky, "was a very energetic woman, but without any medical training, and almost completely illiterate. She could only sign her surname. Probably such cases were not rare then. When I told her that a professor was available here... she waved her hand at me and said no, we cannot allow him to work in the district hospital."

Doctor Barsky went to the chairman of the district executive committee, but got nowhere, then to the secretary of the district party committee. He consulted the head of the district department of the NKVD [People's commissariat for internal affairs. Soviet secret police agency 1934-1943. (tr.)]. They finally decided that despite all, the exiled professor may work in the district hospital under the supervision of comrade Barsky. Doctor Barsky could not take the professor on the hospital staff, so he was forced to pay him 200 rubles on account of vacancies of either hospital cleaners or laundresses. Vladyko Luke could receive patients only under the direction of the chief physician.

The residents of Murtha remember that the exiled bishop lived in poverty, he even did not have enough to eat. "He was not respected." Like the other exiles, vladyko Luke was badly treated.

Surgeon B.I. Khonenko, who worked in Murtha after the war, heard from an old staff member, that the professor had to live in the hospital in a tiny little room next to the kitchen. He lived very modestly. The staff loved him, and the cook Ekaterina Timofeyevna tried to bring some tastier things to the professor, but he asked her not to bring anything. Vladyko Luke wrote to his children: "Don't send money... don't send sweets or food."

The nurse T.I. Starodubtseva recalls, "We, the sisters and nurses, loved him. The professor was not wronged by us."

The nurse of the Murtha hospital remembers the bishop-professor with much love. He spoke openly about his faith, he said: "Wherever they send me there is God." Vladyko Luke walked every morning to some woods that were near and prayed there, putting a folding icon on a tree trunk.

Vladyko Luke wrote a lot, he continued to labour assiduously on "Essays on purulent surgery." In letters to his children he asked them to send him the necessary books, journals, patient histories. He operated not only in Murtha, but also in Krasnoyarsk. His scientific work exhausted him and he considered it indispensable to do regular practical work for half of the day, not to work all day with his brains. [P.]

103   Kliment Yefremovich Voroshilov (1881-1969). [tr.]

104   When the war began the village became empty, the most vital medicines were not there in the hospital, the sisters were forced to wash used bandages. At this time vladyko Luke wrote to his son: "I was trying to send an application to give me work treating casualties, but then I decided to wait with this until the completion of my book, which I will ask to publish urgently, due to the great importance of it for military surgery. In Murtha I found a specialist graphic artist... He made excellent sketches for me..." And again, a month after the beginning of the war: "After finishing the book I will send

an application to the healthcare commissariat and Burdenko, the chief surgeon of the army, to provide me with work as a consultant on treating the wounded..." [P.]

105   ...*I was appointed chief surgeon of evacuation hospital 15-15.*

By God's grace the bishop-professor returned from his place of exile safely. In those terrible times this surprised many people. Soon after the beginning of the war the Murtha recruitment office received an order to use professors in their own field. Vladyko Luke thought they would possibly call him up for the army: "At sixty four years for the first time I will put on a military uniform," he writes.

Initially the bishop received permission to move only to the provincial center, still in the position of an exile, to work in the medical institution.

The former head of the Yenisei steamship line I.M. Nazarov relates that at the beginning of the war vladyko Luke telegraphed the chairman of the presidium of the supreme Soviet, M.I. Kalinin: "I, bishop Luke, professor Voyno-Yasenetsky, serve time in exile according to such-and-such article, in the village of Bolshaya Murtha in Krasnoyarsk province. As a specialist in purulent surgery I can be of help to soldiers at the front or the rear, wherever I will be entrusted to help. I ask you to interrupt my exile and send me to a hospital. When the war is over I am ready to go back into exile. Bishop Luke." When the telegram arrived at the city telegraph office, it was not passed to Moscow, but in accordance with existing orders, it was sent to the provincial committee. In the provincial committee it was discussed at length: to send or not to send. Nazarov saw it lying on the table of the first secretary comrade Golubev. When the issue was discussed there were employees of the NKVD present. They said that professor Voyno-Yasenetsky was a world-famous scholar, that his books were published even in London. In the end it was decided to send the telegram to Kalinin all the same. The answer from Moscow came immediately. The professor was ordered to be taken to Krasnoyarsk.

According to Nazarov several agencies were interested in a good surgeon right away: the hospital for water transport workers, the headquarters of the military district. Krasnoyarsk was to be the eastern boundary for the evacuation of the wounded. An enormous institution was organized there, a MEP (local evacuation center). It consisted of dozens of hospitals and was designed for tens of thousands of hospital beds. The first ambulance echelons already went from the front to Siberia. The MEP needed buildings, linen, food, physicians, and most importantly: qualified scientific supervision. For thousands of versts around there was not a more indispensable and qualified specialist than vladyko Luke, professor Voyno-Yasenetsky.

The chief MEP surgeon arrived in Bolshaya Murthy. He presented to the head of the district MVD [ministry of home affairs (tr.)] a paper according to which the exiled professor Voyno-Yasenetsky was transferred to the local evacuation center, more precisely, to hospital 15-15. Vladyko Luke communicated from Krasnoyarsk: "Tomorrow I will already start to operate." And ten days later: "I was appointed consultant of all Krasnoyarsk province hospitals and I will apparently be released from exile. I was excellently accommodated..."

Vladyko Luke remained in the position of an exile for two years. According to professor Maksimovich he was required to report to the police twice a week. He was allowed to travel to scientific conferences in another city if he had permission of the Chekists and he had to submit reports of his stay there. In the winter of 1942 vladyko Luke lived in the damp cold room which before the war belonged to the school janitor. The bishop seemed to be on the verge of poverty. The hospital kitchen where food was prepared for 1,200 people, was not supposed to give meals to the surgeon-consultant. And since he did not have time to exchange his ration cards for food, nor money to buy food on the black market, he was constantly going without food. The hospital nurses would secretly steal into the janitor's room and leave a plate of gruel on the table. Later vladyko Luke wrote to his son Mikhail: "In the beginning of my work in Krasnoyarsk people had a suspicious attitude towards me."

As in the past, during his prison and exile years, vladyko endured all with deep devotion to God's will. In one of his letters of that time he wrote to his son Mikhail, that he "came to love suffering. It so marvelously cleanses the soul." [P.]

106   *[In evacuation hospital 15-15] I worked for at least two years... The wounded officers and soldiers loved me a lot.*

Former surgeon V.A. Sukhodolskaya recalls: "We, the young surgeons, were able to do very little at the beginning of the war. We looked at Voyno-Yasenetsky with veneration. He taught us a lot. Nobody but him could operate osteomyelitis, and as you know there were thousands of patients with purulence! He taught during operations, and he gave excellent lectures. The lectures were delivered once a week in school № 10." Doctor Branickaya recounts: "In the operating theatre Voyno-Yasenetsky worked quietly, he talked softly with the staff, evenly, concretely. The nurses and assistants were never nervous during his operations."

Besides the fact that bishop Luke operated a lot, he had to give consultations in many hospitals. According to the list of consultations given by the surgeon in three weeks in 1942, the professor was in seven hospitals, examined more than eighty people. Often his examination ended with a note in the document: "Transfer wounded so-and-so to school № 10" (where his hospital was situated).

Vladyko Luke collected the most heavily affected sick and wounded in his hospital. The Krasnoyarsk physician-röntgenologist V.A. Kluge recalls how the surgeon-consultant sent him and other young doctors of hospital 15-15 to the station platform, where ambulance trains were unloaded. He asked to search for wounded with purulent complicated lesions of the hip, the ones most surgeons considered doomed. The reports of hospital 15-15 indicate that many "hopeless" wounded were cured.

By January 1943, all ten thousand beds in the hospitals of MEP-49 were occupied by wounded, and the front sent more and more echelons. Krasnoyarsk was the most distant city the wave of medical evacuation reached. The ambulance trains had to travel seven thousand kilometres, and when they had finally reached the banks of the Yenisei many wounds had started to suppurate, bone injuries had turned into neglected cases of osteomyelitis.

The inspector of all evacuation hospitals, professor Priorov also went to hospital 15-15. He said that he had not seen such excellent results of treating infected injuries of joints as those of vladyko Luke Voyno-Yasenetsky in any other hospital, and he had visited very many hospitals travelling all over the country.

Surgeon V.N. Zinoviev, a student of Voyno-Yasenetsky at hospital 15-15, recalls that vladyko Luke taught his assistants "human surgery." With every wounded he entered into a personal relationship. He remembered every face, knew their surname, and kept in mind all the details of the operation and the postoperative period. Now these words of vladyko Luke have become well-known: "For the surgeon there should not be 'a case' but a living person who is suffering." Manifestations of indifference to one's medical duty outraged bishop Luke.

His labour was sometimes fraught with deep heartfelt suffering. "I take the death of a patient after an operation very hard," wrote bishop Luke to his son. "There were three deaths in the operating theatre, and they positively unsettled me. To you as a theorist these torments are unknown, but I take them harder and harder... I prayed for the deceased at home, there is no church in Krasnoyarsk..."

There also remain stories of Tashkent doctors of how vladyko Luke suffered when someone died in the operating theatre. Obstetrician Antonina Alekseyevna Shorokhova, who worked in Uzbekistan as far back as pre-revolutionary years, recalls: Valentin Felixovich took each of his failures to heart. Once, he was detained at work when all doctors had already left the hospital. For some reason I went to the preoperative surgical department. Suddenly, through the open door of the operating room a voice "from beyond the grave" reached me: "Here's the surgeon who knows no death. And today it is my second..." I turned towards the voice and saw Valentin Felixovich, who looked at me unwaveringly and sorrowfully. I was struck by his depressed posture: he stood bent-over and his hands rested on the edge of the operating table. On the table lay the patient who had died during his operation...

If there was no other way to save a patient vladyko Luke undertook risky operations despite the fact that this put great responsibility on him... When upon entering a ward he noticed that a patient whom he had operated two days ago was not there, he did not ask about anything, walked up to the second floor and locked himself in his room.

A.I. Benyaminovich, a student of the surgeon, recollects about this: "We did not see him in the department then for hours. We knew that each death he considered himself guilty of, caused him deep suffering." Vladyko Luke considered it indispensable *not* to conceal from the dying the proximity of their death, as they might wish to die as a Christian.

The working conditions in the evacuation hospital were also heavy. "Hospital 15-15 falls behind," reported party figures to the provincial committee. "The difficult economic situation of this hospital, the unsatisfactory sanitary condition, the poor quality of the medical work in the departments despite the great capabilities of the qualified specialist professor Voyno-Yasenetsky, and the low work discipline put it in the ranks of bad hospitals..." In a letter to his eldest son vladyko Luke complained that he has to work in intolerable conditions: inept and rude staff, doctors who do not know the basics of surgery. No one was listening to his protests for a year, although he was talking about downright crimes.

"I have come to be very irritable and the other day I suffered such a heavy bout of anger that I had to take a dose of bromide and inject camphor, convulsive gasping arose," writes bishop Luke, "I have never worked in such circumstances."

The surgeon had nearly forty years of experience. All this time he had not come across such a general disorder either in the hospitals of the Russian-Japanese war, or of WW I. Vladyko would get into a state, it happened he even drove out negligent assistants from the operating room. They complained about him. There were trials, the hospital was visited by numerous inspection committees.

All this, of course, was very bad for vladyko's health. During an operation the surgeon would increasingly often have to drop onto a chair, his legs did not keep him up. It was difficult for him to climb the hospital stairs: emphysema [chronic lung disease characterized by their heightened presence of air. (ed.)] made itself felt. But for bishop Luke the more severe grief was the inability to visit the church.

In Krasnoyarsk, a city with thousands of people, the last of a great number of churches had been closed before the war. Hundreds, perhaps thousands of people were deprived of the joy of worship according to vladyko Luke. It is said that believers brought vladyko a lot of icons, and the wall of the janitor's room glittered from icon settings and the light of icon lamps.

In the spring of 1942 the authorities' attitude towards vladyko Luke improved. The surgeon-consultant was given lunch, breakfast and dinner from the shared kitchen, they began to take care to improve his working conditions. In Irkutsk, at an inter-provincial meeting of chief surgeons there was "a real triumph" for archbishop Luke, as he wrote to Mikhail. "The opinion of me in the ruling circles is the highest and there is complete confidence. Thank God!"

Vladyko Luke made a number of new discoveries, his operations, lectures, conference papers were appreciated by doctors, lecturers and professors. "I am much honoured: when I come in at major meetings of employees or commanding officers, all rise," bishop Luke wrote at that time.

About this time of his life vladyko Luke wrote to N.P. Puzin, whom he had met on his arrival in Krasnoyarsk [Memories of N.P. Puzin of archbishop Luke and letters of vladyko to him are published in "Herald of the Russian Christian movement" № 170, 1994 (ed.)]:

June 20th, 1942

Dear Nicolai Pavlovich,

Also I'm sorry that you left Krasnoyarsk. With metropolitan Sergius I started a voluminous correspondence on religious-philosophical, church-political and tactical questions which would be very interesting to you. Of course, I cannot transmit this correspondence to you.

I have one big sorrow: from Novosibirsk I was told that they cannot publish my book for lack of paper... I am taken care of exclusively: commanding officers from among the patients called the director of the shoe factory, ordered him to make shoes to measure for me, and by all means to get rubber boots for operations. Also they ordered two sets of linen, two towels, handkerchiefs. They reprimand the sisters if they see that I myself carry a plate. The MEP, the revolutionary military council, nominated me for an award, apparently for an order. Truly a rapid evolution from a persona odiosa to a persona grata! Thank God!

They feed me so abundantly that I give away half of it to the people around me and to acquaintances. And the poor renovationist bishop in Murtha is starving to the point of getting famine oedemas because he has to live on only 400 grams of bread. Tomorrow I move into a new apartment (where the

pharmacy was). There will be the best conditions for reflection on religious themes, which I am occupied with now, complete isolation, silence, peace, solitude.
May God bless and preserve you,
Archbishop Luke

December 25th, 1942
Rejoice in the Lord, Nikolai,
...For the last four weeks already I do not work due to very heavy overwork, mostly cerebral. I lay for three weeks in the hospital of the provincial committee, now I am lying at home in my own apartment. The doctors say that until I am recovered, I should not work more than four hours and do no more than two operations. And so far I've worked up to eight-nine hours, and did four-five operations.
...My intensive correspondence with metropolitan Sergius continues.
May God help you endure the burdens of war time and bless you,
Archbishop Luke

At this time, vladyko Luke was called by the first secretary of the provincial party committee, and he was told that the relationship between the church and the state would soon improve, and he could return to episcopal ministry. By the grace of God, after a while vladyko was indeed appointed to the Krasnoyarsk cathedra, and his preaching about Christ was heard again.
"They promised to open a church long ago, but everyone is still procrastinating, and again I will remain without a service on the great feast of Christmas," writes the bishop with sorrow to his son Mikhail at the end of 1942, and finally, on March 5th, he reports: "The Lord sent me unspeakable joy. After sixteen years of agonizing longing for the church and silence the Lord opened my mouth again. A small church in Nikolayevka, a suburb of Krasnoyarsk, has opened, and I am appointed archbishop of Krasnoyarsk... Of course, I will continue to work in the hospital, there is no obstacle to that at all."

Vladyko Luke wrote: "Few people knew about the first service, but still about two hundred people came. Many were standing in the yard."

"The first service... immediately very much improved my nervous state, but my neurasthenia was so severe that neuropathologists prescribed me complete rest for two weeks. I did not take a rest and I am sure I can do without it," writes vladyko Luke.

A month later he confirms: "Since the opening of the church my neurosis has completely gone and my capacity for work has been restored."

Once again at the door of the apartment of the archbishop appears a plate announcing that for church matters he receives people on Tuesdays and Fridays from six to eight in the evening. Vladyko Luke writes to N.P. Puzin:

For a long time I could not answer you for two reasons:

1) I was extremely busy rushing to finish my monograph on late resections on gunshot injuries of joints.

2) I felt very bad and sometimes kept to my bed for whole days due to severe cerebral overwork. This state of exhaustion lasted for nearly four months... They require that I won't go to church if I do not work in the hospital. So I force myself to work.

To the tiny cemetery church in Nikolayevka it is a half hour walk. It is a big climb uphill, and I get tired to exhaustion. The church is so small that it properly fits forty-fifty people, but two to three hundred come, and it is difficult to walk to the altar, as at Easter.

We only would be able to serve the priestly rite there, but also that is not yet possible, because there are no vestments. By all appearances we will get them from the theatre. There is no deacon, no choristers, even no reader. A seventy three year old archpriest serves, and I preach. This is for me and for the people a great joy.

There is great hope that in spring they will open the Intercession church (at the corner of Stalin street and Surikov street)...

His beatitude was dangerously ill with pneumonia, but thank God he has recovered. He was sick for a long time so he did not write to me. I wish you success in your work, health and salvation of your soul.

A. L., 17.03.1943

In the church in Nikolayevka episcopal services turned out to be impossible. The authorities promised to open a second church, but only after a year. "In the theatre there are many episcopal vestments, but they do not give them to us. They consider it more important to dress actors in them. They cut them up to alter them to have a comic effect," wrote vladyko Luke.

Subsequently he obtained episcopal vestments in Novosibirsk, where he had presented a paper at a conference of surgeons of military hospitals. In Krasnoyarsk another church was opened after some time.

The archbishop wrote at that time in a letter that the government's attitude to the church had changed dramatically: "...Everywhere churches are opened and they are repaired at the expense of the city councils. Bishops are appointed." And about himself: "Remember, Mikhail, that my monkhood with its vows, my title, and my service to God are for me the most sacred and my foremost duty. I have truly and deeply renounced the world and medical fame. My fame, of course, could become very great, but for me it is worth nothing now. And in the service of God is all my joy, my whole life, for my faith is deep. However, I also do not intend to give up my medical and scientific work."

After a few months he conveys to Mikhail:

In Krasnoyarsk, in "circles" they said about me: "Let him serve, it is politically necessary." I wrote to you that there was an authoritative order not to prosecute me for my religious convictions. Even if the status of the church had not changed so much, if my high scientific value did not protect me, I would not hesitate to walk the path of active service to the church again. Because you, my children, do not need my help, and I have become used to prison and exiles and I do not fear them.

...Oh, if you only knew how stupid and limited atheism is, and how alive real communion with God for those who love Him...

The day that marked the twentieth anniversary of his ordination as a bishop vladyko Luke wrote to his eldest son. He recalled the journey long ago from Tashkent to Panjakent: "It was the beginning of the thorny path I was to go. But it was the path of glory and of God. I believe that my suffering has come to an end..."

Archbishop Luke put a lot of efforts into the publication of the second edition of "Essays on purulent surgery." He knew that the book would bring great practical benefit to doctors, that the book was needed. In 1943, he was finally able to get permission to publish it, as he writes to N.P. Puzin:

July 1st, 1943

Nikolai Pavlovich, peace and blessings,

I have great, happy news. On May 2nd I sent a letter to Stalin about my book, with an appendix with reviews by professor Manuylov and Priorov who praise the book to the skies. The result: a letter from Medgiz [State medical publishing house (tr.)] of June 26th with the request to send the manuscript for publication. And the monograph about joints, that the local provincial publishing house was slow to publish, they also request I send to Moscow. Towards the winter the book and the monograph will come out.

Our hospital has been reduced to two hundred and fifty beds, and the work has become less. They do not want to open the church in the city, and from Tashkent they write that a renovationist bishop arrived there, and for him they open a lot of churches... And in autumn and spring it is impossible to walk to Nikolayevka. I recently went there after rain, but I fell in the mud and I returned. My health, thank God, is good. I recently received thanks and a letter of recommendation from the military council of the Siberian military district.

Be healthy and prosperous. May the Lord preserve you,

Archbishop Luke, 01.07.1943

Nikolai Pavlovich, peace and blessings,

I have big and unexpected news. March 2nd I received a telegram from Moscow. The All-Slavic committee asks me to write an article for the foreign Slavic press about my public activities during the patriotic war [WW II (tr.)] as archbishop of Krasnoyarsk and surgeon of the red army hospitals. You, of course, are able to fully appreciate the significance of this proposal and its possible great consequences. Within two days I will send the article. However I don't have time to copy it for you.

I serve and preach every holiday and every Sunday. The work in the hospital is as before... My neurosis recurs from time to time, and on August 8th, I could not even serve the liturgy because of it.

Furunculosis, from which you suffer, can most likely only be cured with an autovaccine.

May the Lord help you and bless you,

Archbishop Luke, 16.08.1943

About his correspondence with the locum tenens of the patriarchal throne metropolitan Sergius vladyko Luke recalled: "In 1942 I had an intensive correspondence with him on major issues of modern life, and his letters often amazed me by their depth, by their correctness of understanding the essence of Christianity, by their knowledge of the sacred Scripture and church history. Some of them can even be called small theological treatises. He did not agree with me about everything, and often I had to admit he was absolutely right."

The correspondence of metropolitan Sergius and archbishop Luke was of no small importance for the preparation of the council of bishops of the Russian orthodox church in 1943. Archbishop Luke took an active part in drawing up the documents of the council. He was a member of the holy synod.

After metropolitan Sergius became patriarch, he attracted vladyko Luke to participate in the "Journal of the Moscow patriarchate." This collaboration with the JMP lasted ten years. [P.]

107   *At the end of my exile in 1943 I returned to Moscow and was appointed to Tambov.*

At the end of his exile bishop Luke began to try to be transferred away from Siberia. The Krasnoyarsk officials did not want to let him go. Both civil and military authorities tried to please him. In the list of best doctors of the province Voyno-Yasenetsky's name was at the top. The transfer problem was being agreed upon between the patriarchate and the people's healthcare commissariat for several months. Finally people's commissar Tretyakov telegraphed: "We intend to transfer you to Tambov, a wide field of activity and a large hospital." Most holy patriarch Sergius by a special decree appointed bishop Luke archbishop of Tambov and Michurinsk. In early 1944, bishop Luke moved to Tambov.

A lot of work was awaiting the archbishop in his new eparchy. He continued to combine archpastoral service and serving his fellow human beings with medical work.

"Not a bad-looking city, the look of an old provincial town is almost completely preserved," wrote vladyko Luke to his son. "They received me very well here... At the request of the presidium (surgical society) I have made a report on osteomyelitis at the district conference of the Orlov military district. I spoke and sat in the presidium in my cassock, with a cross and a panagia."

Candidate of medicine [Ph.D. (tr.)] V.A. Polyakov recalls a meeting with vladyko Luke (in the surgeons' assembly) in 1944: "At the meeting there were a lot of people. At the table of the presidium the chairman had already risen to announce the title of a paper. But suddenly the doors opened wide and a gigantic man with spectacles entered the hall. His gray hair flowed down to his shoulders. His light, transparent, white lacy beard rested on his chest. The lips under his mustache were tightly pressed. His large white hands fingered a black prayer rope. The man walked slowly into the room and sat in the front row. The chairman asked him to take place in the presidium. He got up, walked to the stage and sat in the chair offered to him. It was professor Valentin Felixovich Voyno-Yasenetsky..."

Administering the eparchy archbishop Luke immediately faced many difficulties. For many years the Tambov church housed under its roof a workers' dormitory. It was reduced to the last degree of desolation. Its inhabitants had hacked the icons, they had broken and discarded the iconostasis and they had covered the walls with abusive language. Vladyko Luke accepted the inheritance of the atheists without complaints and began to repair the church, assemble the clergy of the parish, and conduct services whilst continuing his medical work. Under the care of the archbishop of Tambov there were now hundred and fifty hospitals, with five hundred to a thousand beds in each. He also gave consultations to the large surgical department of the big city hospital. Vladyko Luke was still willing to work day and night, despite the fact that soon he was about to turn 70.

"We bring the church into a state of grandeur... The work at the hospital is going well... I lecture to physicians about purulent arthritis... There are almost no free days. On Saturdays I receive patients for two hours in the clinic. At home I do not receive patients, because that is quite beyond my strength by now. But patients, especially villagers coming from far away, do not understand this and call me a merciless bishop. This is very hard for me. In exceptional circumstances I have to receive patients at home," he wrote to his son and his family.

O.V. Streltsova, a retired teacher from Tambov, describes the following event from what she had heard from her late friend doctor V.P. Dmitryevskaya:

Once, when vladyko Luke in the capacity of doctor made his round of red army patients in the hospital, one sick soldier allowed himself to offend him, saying: "What is this longhaired person walking around here for?" And what happened? That very same evening the offender was punished and brought to his senses. At twelve o'clock at night he had a deadly attack that made him understand, and he, the patient, asked the doctor to call the professor, i.e., vladyko Luke, to see him. He came at night, entered the ward and went to the patient. The patient tearfully apologized to the bishop-doctor for his offense and begged him to save his life, because he already felt death approaching. Vladyko Luke commanded to immediately prepare everything for an emergency operation. They brought in the patient, prepared for the operation. Vladyko, as he usually did in such cases, asked the patient whether he believed in God, because not the professor will restore his life, but God through the hands of the doctor.

The patient could not stop his tears, said that now he believes and he realizes that he paid for his rude mockery of the bishop. The vladyko-professor did a very serious emergency operation, returned the patient back to life. This event had a strong effect on all hospital patients.

At the time vladyko Luke arrived in Tambov, his eyesight was already severely weakened. Now he no longer always succeeded in making those delicate incisions that gave rise to admiration in the past. Due to the deterioration of his eyesight vladyko had to refrain from the most complicated operations. Many testimonies have been preserved that people truly loved vladyko Luke: the congregation loved him, his colleagues loved him, patients - often not religious - loved him. The parishioners of the Tambov cathedral remember their vladyko with warm love and gratitude. Here are three reminiscences:

1) He came to us at the very beginning of 1944. But first, he had no vestments for the services. They sent him a sacerdotal robe before Lent. He served for the first time and addressed the faithful with a short word: "After long spiritual starvation we can meet again, and thank God... I am appointed to be your pastor." Then he blessed each person in the church.
2) Vladyko started the day with a book and with a book - of prayer at that - he ended the day. The nun Lyubov left him a library, she was one of the princely family Shirinsky-Shikhmatov, who lived in exile in Tambov.
3) A widow stood beside the church when vladyko came to the service. "Why are you, sister, standing there so sadly?" Vladyko asked. And she told him: "I have five small children, and our little house is completely falling apart." "Well, wait till the end of the service, I want to talk with you." After the service, he took the widow home and inquired what bad things had happened to her and he gave her money to build a house. Olga Vladimirovna Streltsova recalls that the vladyko's sermons attracted many doctors, librarians and teachers to the church. The sermons in the church were written down by an English teacher, who was very dedicated to archbishop Luke, Natalia Mikhailovna Fyodorova. After that another parishioner-typist typed the sermons on cigarette paper and distributed them to the believers. Seventy-seven sermons were written down in Tambov.
Archdeacon father Vasily Malin, whom bishop Luke ordained a deacon in 1945, narrates: "There was an old man among the parishioners, a cashier, I.M. Fomin. He read the hours in the choir. He read poorly, incorrectly pronounced the words. Vladyko corrected him repeatedly. One day after the service, when archbishop Luke explained to him for the fifth or sixth time how to pronounce some of the Church Slavonic expressions, they got into an argument. Vladyko Luke temperamentally gestured with a liturgical book, and obviously offended Fomin. He was indignant and said that the bishop had hit him, and demonstratively stopped attending the church. After some time had passed vladyko put on a cross and a panagia and set out to the offended parishioner to apologize. He had to walk across the whole city. Fomin did not receive the archbishop. Vladyko went to him again and again he did not receive forgiveness. The cashier literally humiliated him.

He forgave vladyko only a few days before the archbishop left Tambov."

The teacher Sofia Ivanovna Borisova preserved very interesting memories of vladyko Luke. She was German by birth, Lutheran, and at the time archbishop Luke stayed in Tambov she wanted to convert to orthodoxy. Vladyko took her home, talked with her and prepared her to convert to the orthodox faith. She became very close to him and after the departure of vladyko Luke to Simferopol she corresponded with him for a long time.

In late 1944, in one of his sermons vladyko said that the German brutalities were not accidental, that cruelty was inherent to the German people as a whole. This national trait the Germans had repeatedly revealed in the last century and reflects, so to say, the spirit of the German people. Sofia Ivanovna was hurt by these words. She overcame her embarrassment and after the sermon she went up to the archbishop and told him that there are all sorts of Germans as well as Russians and she doesn't know of any cruel German spirit. Vladyko Luke listened to her without a word and left the church also without a word. But a few days later when there was a huge gathering he told the congregation that he had found an unacceptable mistake in his last sermon. It is incorrect to speak of a cruel nature of all Germans in general. He asks those who were offended by this remark to forgive him if they can. In future he will think over his sermons more seriously.

[In Soviet documents it says that the great church was blown up by the Germans. In reality it wasn't. During the retreat it was mined with a time bomb by the red army. The Germans tried unsuccessfully to clear the great church of mines, but they could not do it. There was an explosion. In fact the Germans were trying to gain popularity and credibility, so with rare exceptions they did not touch the orthodox churches. On the contrary, numerous cases are known of the Germans opening churches. We know the attitude to national holy places of the atheistic political officers of the red army. One witness, hegumen Mikhail, says: "Already when the Germans had retreated from our village near Volokolamsk only a few dozens of kilometers a car arrived with red army miners. They immediately headed for the church. For a long time they were digging something, drilling, and they carried some cases. At four o'clock in the morning there was an explosion. The ancient beautiful church was turned into a heap of ruins. The car immediately left. The next day, it was announced to the villagers that the church was blown up by... the Germans." Apparently, there was an unspoken directive to destroy the churches in areas liberated from the Germans. (ed.)]

Those who knew vladyko Luke noted that he trusted people a lot.

Archbishop Innokentiy Kalinin (Leoferov), who was eparchial secretary of vladyko Luke in Tambov, recalled:

He was very truthful. Vladyko Luke was truthful to the point that it became funny. He supposed that everybody around him was as truthful. But people, you yourself know... When he left from Tambov, I accompanied him on the train until Michurinsk. We were alone in the compartment, and vladyko asked:

"Tell me, what is the biggest vice I should avoid?"

"Please, do not trust slanderers," I said. "In reaction to the complaints of liars you, your eminence, sometimes punish people who are not guilty of anything."

"Yes?" He was amazed. And then, on reflection, he added: "With this I cannot part. I cannot not trust people."

Archbishop Luke tried to get the city's cathedral handed over to the believers. Immediately after his arrival in Tambov, he wrote to his son: "Almost certainly they will give us the big two-story cathedral." In May, he wrote: "Moscow has refused to open our cathedral, and it is a great disappointment to me." Karpov later promised vladyko Luke to open the cathedral or another large church in Tambov, but the Tambov commissioner of orthodox church affairs refused. In August, bishop Luke reports: "The cathedral will be opened only if the believers petition for it, but up to now there have been no initiators, everyone is afraid."

Karpov really wanted to open the cathedral in Tambov, but Kozyrkov, the chairman of the provincial executive committee at the time, and Volkov, the first secretary of the provincial party committee – both Komsomol members of the twenties – resisted this in every way possible. Kozyrkov died before long (vladyko Luke diagnosed him with inoperable cancer of the stomach), but Volkov until the end of the war never allowed a second church to be opened in the city. And after the war this question was no longer considered in Moscow.

Kozyrkov did not treat vladyko Luke badly, he considered him a doctor who had accidentally been caught in the "church whirlpool." One day he invited vladyko to his office, and wishing to express his disposition he said:

"How can we award you for your excellent work in the hospital?"

"Open the city's cathedral."

"Well, no, the cathedral you will never see."

"But there is nothing else I need from you," the archbishop said, and he left the provincial executive committee.

With the new chairman who replaced Kozyrkov archbishop Luke had the following incident. In late 1945, the bishop and his secretary were invited to the provincial executive committee to award them medals "For valiant labour in the great patriotic war of 1941-1945." After presenting the medals the chairman said that although the work of Voyno-Yasenetsky as a consultant of the evacuation hospital was completed (these hospitals left Tambov in the autumn of 1944 and moved further to the west), he hoped that the professor would continue to share his vast experience with the medics of the city.

Archbishop Luke replied the following: "I have taught and I am prepared to teach doctors what I know. I brought back to life and health hundreds, perhaps thousands of wounded and probably I would have helped still more if you (he emphasized this 'you' to have the audience understand that he uses the word in a wide sense) had not arrested me for no reason at all, and had not dragged me to prisons and on exiles for eleven years. That's how much time has been lost and how many people were not saved. This happened by no means of my will."

The provincial authorities were shocked by these words. For some time an oppressive silence reigned on the podium and in the audience. Somehow the chairman came to himself. He babbled to say it is time to forget the past, and that we must live in the present and the future. And here again the bass voice of vladyko Luke resounded: "Well, no, sorry, I will never forget!"

After the death of patriarch Sergius preparations began for the local council of the Russian orthodox church and the election of a new patriarch. Vladyko Luke was present in Moscow at the meeting of the bishops, held on November 21st, 1944 for the election of a pre-council committee. Archbishop Luke reminded those present of the election procedure of the patriarch by lot, which was developed at the local council in 1917. According to the resolution of that council, the nomination of patriarchal candidates must be done by the participants of the council and the vote should be secret. Vladyko Luke announced that, since metropolitan Aleksey was the only patriarchal candidate nominated, that resolution was violated, so he would vote against metropolitan Aleksey. As a result, vladyko Luke was the only Russian bishop who was not invited to the council at which 41 Russian and 5 foreign bishops took part. [P.]

108   *In 1946 I was awarded the Stalin prize first class for my "Essays on purulent surgery" and "Late resections on infected wounds of large joints."*

"A lot of congratulations from everywhere," wrote vladyko Luke after receiving the prize, "from the patriarch, metropolitans, bishops, Karpov (chairman of the council of ROC affairs), Mityarev, Tretyakov, the academy of medical sciences, the committee of secondary education affairs, the institute of theology, professors and so on and so forth. They praise my work extraordinarily high... My fame is a great triumph for the church, the patriarch telegraphed." Almost the entire prize his eminence Luke donated to orphans who were victims of the war.

Vladyko Luke treated patients for God's sake. In praise of God he also often helped those who lived in misery and comforted the unfortunate. Appointments at home and private consultations were free. And his scientific work, the publication of books and articles, and receiving the state prize vladyko Luke considered as a means to increase the authority of the church. There is no doubt that in those terrible times a famous scientist, a renowned surgeon, who was openly preaching about Christ could compel many, many people to think.

Vladyko Luke believed that his scientific work would attract many intellectuals to orthodoxy. And so it did. In a broadcast of radio station BBC at that time it was reported that a group of young French men and women converted to orthodoxy. They referred in their declaration to Christian scientists in the USSR: Ivan Pavlov, Vladimir Filatov and archbishop Luke Voyno-Yasenetsky.

"Today my opinion was confirmed that I am a considerable trump card for our government," vladyko Luke writes to his son. "A TASS [news agency (tr.)] correspondent was especially sent to take photographs of me for the foreign press. And earlier the patriarchate asked me to send a biography for the Journal of the patriarchate and for the information bureau. Two local artists paint my portrait. The archbishop of Yaroslavl has just returned from America and there he already read reports in the newspapers about me, about an archbishop-laureate of the Stalin Prize... Tomorrow a sculptor will come from Moscow to sculpt my bust..."

In February 1945 patriarch Aleksey awarded archbishop Luke of Tambov and Michurinsk the right to wear a diamond cross on his klobuk [headgear of Orthodox monks (tr.)] for his great services to the Russian church.

In the Tambov eparchy vladyko Luke restored and consecrated several churches. He focused his efforts on the restoration of parish life. The divine services which were conducted by archbishop Luke were of high spirituality and prayer. He spent a lot of efforts educating the congregation. "There I preached a good deal and I instilled in everyone a great love for venerable Seraphim, so after each service all the people were singing a troparion to him before his icon)," said archbishop Luke in a sermon on the feast day of Saint Seraphim of Sarov.

In 1946, vladyko Luke was once and for all forbidden to speak to scientific audiences in a cassock with a cross and panagia. He wrote to his son: "I got an offer of the USSR people's healthcare commissar to deliver a main lecture on late resections of large joints at a big congress, where the results of military surgical work are to be summed up. I readily agreed, but I wrote that the people's commissar forbids me to speak in a cassock, and the patriarch - without a cassock. I wrote to the patriarch about this, he replied to me in a letter... his opinion coincides with mine: to speak in civilian clothes and to hide my hair at a meeting where everyone knows that I am a bishop would mean that I am ashamed of my sacred dignity. If an assembly considers the presence of a bishop unacceptable and even offensive, then a bishop should disdain to speak before such an assembly... I spoke on the telephone with the organizer of the congress, doctor Dedovy. He got upset and said that everyone including the people's commissar attaches great importance to my lecture and he promised all superiors would stand up for me. But after one day he said that the superiors had been occupied all day with this issue, they had talked with Tretyakov and Karpov, and allegedly the case reached the ears of the central party committee, but they did not agree to me speaking in a cassock. I asked him to tell the commissar, that I take this as being excluded from the community of scientists." [P.]

109   *In May 1946 I was appointed archbishop of Simferopol and Crimea.*

At this time, all the trials of his difficult life and the effects of exceptionally strenuous work increasingly affected the health of archbishop Luke. He lost his eyesight, his heart increasingly often failed: arrhythmia, decompensation. He writes: "The grief and tears of the (Tambov) flock that loved me so warmly upset me, and again my heart became worse. Yesterday and today, on Thomas Sunday [Sunday after Easter (tr.)], I did not serve."

In May 1946 vladyko moved to Crimea. "However much my Tambov flock was crying, however much they requested the patriarchate to keep me in Tambov, I had to go to Simferopol. This was undoubtedly the will of God, for here I am very much needed. I have to put a ravaged eparchy in order."

The war had wounded the Crimea terribly. Cities were destroyed, villages turned into ashes. At the place of a great number of Crimean churches there was a ruin now. In Chersonesus, ancient Korsun, where saint Prince Vladimir was baptized, the majestic cathedral of Vladimir equal-to-the-apostles was destroyed. Archbishop Luke put a lot of work in restoring churches and resuming church services in them. The economic situation was very difficult. A quarter of a loaf of bread cost fifty rubles on the market. Housewives bought cereal from farmers per fifty gram cup. They carried it in little bags as extremely valuable. The episcopal apartment in Hospital street occupied the second floor of an old house that had not been renovated for a long time. Apart from the bishop and his eparchial office, there also lived some other families on the same floor. There were bugs in the house. In the mornings a queue was formed at the one tap in the house.

Vladyko Luke was ready to help everyone. In the bishop's kitchen lunch was cooked for 15-20 people. Lunches were unpretentious, they consisted of soup alone, but in 1946-1948 many people in Simferopol did not even have such food. "Many hungry children, lonely old women, and poor people who were lacking means of subsistence came for lunch," remembers the niece of archbishop Luke, Vera Prozorovskaya. "Every day I cooked a big pot, and they raked it out to the bottom. In the evening my uncle asked, 'How was it today at the table? Did you feed everyone? Was there enough for everybody?'"

Vladyko Luke himself ate very simply. Breakfast consisted of one dish. If they gave a second dish he would become angry. He dressed very modestly. Simferopol teacher Yudina, whom vladyko had given money to buy a house, recalls that his eminence always wore patched cassocks with torn elbows. Every time his niece Vera offered to sew him new clothes, she got to hear as an answer: "Patch them up, patch them up, Vera, there are a lot of poor people." There were really a lot of poor people around. The eparchial secretary maintained a long list of people in need. At the end of each month 30-40 money orders were sent to people on these lists.

The state of affairs in the Crimean eparchy was complex. Vladyko Luke started to go around the fifty eight Crimean parishes. The majority of the churches were opened relatively recently (before the war there was only one single open church for the entire Crimea). In the parishes they complained to the bishop about the lack of basic necessities: vestments, liturgical books, incense, candles, lamp oil.

Vladyko took it especially hard when he saw that not all pastors were a worthy example for the believers. He did not tire repeating to them: "How will I answer God for all of you?" The former secretary of the eparchial office of Crimea, father Vitaly Karwowski, remembers that his eminence's indignation was not only provoked by priests who drank, but also by those who smoked. So he prescribed severe penances, he would ban clergy to serve in the church for three months. Just as he would demand categorically that the priests were always and everywhere in clothing corresponding to their rank. "He that is unjust in the least is unjust also in much (Lk. 16:10)," he quoted the Gospel and he would punish priests who shaved their beard and cut their hair short. Some of them avoided to comply with the requirements of the bishop. But vladyko Luke remained unbending.

In the eparchial archives the following epistle of 1947 has been preserved:

Recently, I came across a tattered liturgy book of a priest. All the bottom corners of the pages were black with dirt. Oh my God! That means that this priest lacks fear of God, because he took the Body of Christ in his dirty hands, with black dirt under his nails! Of course it is a shame if a priest does not wash himself, if he is dressed in dirty clothes, if he stands in front of the holy throne in galoshes.

...In our eparchy the priests already do not shave and cut their hair, but how many still do so in other places! How many also are ashamed to wear spiritual clothes and dress according to fashion no different from the laity! And already a long, long time ago the great writer of the Russian land Nikolai Gogol wrote about spiritual clothes: "It is good that even by their very clothes that do not conform to the changes and whims of our foolish fashion, they (the clergy) differ from us. Their garments are beautiful and majestic. They are not meaningless rococo remaining from the eighteenth century nor patchwork that doesn't explain anything, like that of the Roman catholic priests. They have meaning, they have the image and likeness of the clothes worn by the Saviour Himself...

Here's another epistle of the archpastor to the priests of his eparchy: "Are there many priests among you who are like an earnest doctor? Do you know how much effort and attention kind and experienced doctors devote to seriously ill patients? ...But you know that the task of a doctor is only to treat *bodily* diseases, and our task is immeasurably more important. After all, God appointed us to the great cause of healing *souls*, of deliverance from the eternal torments!..."

Vladyko Luke forbids a priest from serving if he violates the canonical rules of worship: if he burns incense in a cold censer, if he doesn't perform the sacrament of baptism according to the rules, if he uses surrogates incense instead of labdanum, etc.. He reminds them of the terrible words of the prophet Jeremiah, who said, "Cursed be he that doeth the work of the Lord deceitfully." [Jer. 48:10. (ed.)]

In one of his epistles archbishop Luke specifies with sorrow cases of money-grabbing. He gives the names of those who turn the priesthood into a source of personal enrichment: "What should I do with such a priest? I'll try to shame him, to touch the best parts of his heart, I'll transfer him to another parish with the stern warning, that if he does not correct his ways, he'll be dismissed from the staff and I'll wait if the Lord will send a good shepherd in his place" [JMP 1948, № 6, p. 8 (ed.)].

Zealously labouring for the strictness of the believers, vladyko Luke says in an eparchial decree: "Declare to all priests that Christians who in former days faint-heartedly declared themselves to be unbelievers in questionnaires, should be considered apostates from Christ (Matt. 10: 33). They should be forbidden communion for four years" (Eparchial decree № 16-1, 24.01.1947).

"Indulgence to sinners, assigning soft penances (bows, etc.) are considered necessary to make allowance for the weakness of the people of our times. And this is deeply wrong. And it is correct to exert influence on spiritually weak people precisely by the severity of confession, the fear of God. We must shake up their hearts. Are people ashamed when they don't get permission [to partake in holy Communion (tr.)]? This shame is necessary for them and their salvation, and we must not cowardly free them from this shame to please them... I remind priests who consider it desirable to maintain the former practice of using only light penances, that they ought to carry out the instructions of their bishop without criticism, for God has entrusted the bishop with the responsibility for his flock in the eparchy and with the guidance of all priests..." (Eparchial decree № 16-7, 07.06.1947).

At this time, they again began closing churches everywhere. To create an outward appearance of legality of these actions, the KGB developed a set of rules by which a church could be closed. One of them said that a church is to be closed, if it has no priest for six months. There were not enough priests in the Crimea as in the rest of the country, and towards the autumn of 1949 the authorized representative of Simferopol put out the icon lamps in the church of the town of Stary Krym, and then in the villages Zhelyabovka and Besharan. The churches of some more settlements of the Crimea were at risk.

Vladyko Luke tried his best to save churches. He transferred priests to empty churches, sent them out of the cities to the villages. Some priests were displeased with this. The archbishop wrote in an epistle to all the priests and deacons of the Simferopol eparchy: "Could military personnel possibly refuse to be transferred to another part of the military? Would a civil servant dare to refuse transfer to another service, even if these transfers and assignments painfully affected his personal and family interests? Indeed why is this also not possible in the church? If a harsh military discipline is completely indispensable in the army, it is even more necessary in the church, which has an even more important task than that of the armed forces to protect our fatherland, because the church has the task to protect and save human souls."

Archbishop Luke tried to bring clergy from other provinces of the country to the Crimea. But also here he was obstructed: the police did not register the newcomers. The commissioner put together "a case" now against one, then against another priest, and demanded that the bishop dismissed those who had fallen out of favour. Vladyko Luke protected deserving pastors by all possible means. Whatever cause the archbishop blessed, the commissioner immediately annulled it. This struggle lasted for years.

Archbishop Luke wrote sorrowfully to patriarch Aleksey about the situation in the villages of the eparchy: "On Sundays and even holidays churches and prayer houses are almost empty. People have lost the habit to worship and somehow only ceremonial faith remains. People almost forgot about holy matrimony, about the funeral service for the dead. There are a lot of unbaptized children. At the same time, it is the general view of the priests that you can't possibly say people are losing faith. The reason for the alienation of people from the church, from worship and sermons, lies in the fact that believers are deprived of the possibility to attend services, because on Sundays and even on the great feasts they are forced to carry out work at the kolkhoz [collective farm (tr.)] or drawn away from the church by an order to bring cattle to the vet for examination, by a device called 'little Sundays' [voluntary unpaid work on Sunday (tr.)]... This plight of the church can only be changed by resolute measures of the central government."

It is well-known that on the part of the most holy patriarch Aleksey with respect to archbishop Luke there was some caution. Nevertheless, vladyko Luke always had an attitude of complete obedience to the highest church authority. "The patriarch should not be judged, he should be pitied," he wrote in a letter. And in one of his sermons archbishop Luke fervently urges the flock to always have a deep respect for the most holy patriarch, to remember the great labours and sufferings that were his lot.

In 1948, the orthodox church celebrated the quincentenary of its autocephaly, but archbishop Luke was not invited to Moscow. He wrote: "Many eparchial bishops were invited to a very important congress of representatives of all orthodox churches, but not me. This conclusively proves that it has been ordered [by the KGB (ed.)] to keep me away." When vladyko Luke was refused to be transferred to Odessa instead of the Crimea, he wrote that the most holy patriarch Aleksey "has no power," "after my eleven-year anamnesis my place can only be in some poky hole of a place."

Some testimonies of those close to archbishop Luke have also been preserved about his humility and non-possessiveness. In 1951, vladyko went to Odessa, where the most holy patriarch was on holiday at his dacha. Sofia Sergeyevna Beletskaya wrote to vladyko's daughter: "Unfortunately, papa is again dressed very badly: in his old canvas cassock and a very old inside rason from cheap fabric. I had to wash both for the trip to the patriarch. Here, all of the higher clergy are well dressed: expensive beautiful cassocks and perfectly sewn rasons, and papa – such a remarkable man – is dressed worst of all, it just is a shame..."

At this time, vladyko Luke was less and less engaged in medical activities. "My surgery is fading away, and big church challenges are arising," he wrote to his eldest son. In another letter he said: "Surgery is not compatible with the episcopal ministry, as both the one and the other require the whole person, all your energy, all your time, and the patriarch writes that I have to give up surgery."

Shortly before he left Tambov vladyko Luke wrote: "My heart is bad, and all professors and doctors who examined it consider it absolutely necessary for me to give up active surgery." When archbishop Luke moved to the Crimea, the director of the Simferopol medical institute and its scientific council considered it better to pretend that they did not know about his arrival. Medical students who met archbishop Luke in Simferopol with flowers were punished for this.

In early 1947, the bishop wrote to his son:

My lectures at the surgical society and at two doctors' congresses were a great success. At the society all stood up when I entered. This, of course, many did not like. They started to obstruct me. They made it clear to me that I should not give lectures in episcopal attire any more. In Alushta my paper was torn up (at the request of physicians!)...

I had agreed to lecture twice a month on contaminated surgery and to guide the work of doctors in surgical clinics. This they frustrated also. Then I stopped going to the surgical society.

But at the same time vladyko announced he would give free medical consultations, and hundreds of patients from all over the Crimea rushed to the second floor of the bishop's house in Hospital street.

Apart from church services, sermons, reception of patients and administrative work for the eparchy, in 1949 bishop Luke was collecting material for his monograph, a revision of his dissertation "Local anesthesia," which was to bring surgeons undeniable benefit.

The military doctors of Simferopol sent archbishop Luke their representative M.F. Averchenko with the request to share with them his medical expertise. Vladyko happily agreed to give consultations in their hospital. For the arrival of the consultant all branches of the hospital usually prepared the most severely diseased patients. But in June 1951 vladyko Luke wrote: "I was banned from surgery because of my episcopal rank, and they are not even inviting me any more for consultations. Because of this, patients with severe purulence will die..."

Vladyko Luke was on friendly terms with academician V.P. Filatov, a deeply religious man. Filatov received Valentin Voyno-Yasenetsky in his institute, and he treated the diseased eye of archbishop Luke. The metropolitan wrote to his son Aleksey, "Filatov... is a very nice person, religious in all respects. I visited him twice, and he came to my hotel for confession." And in another letter: "With Filatov I had a long conversation about his scientific work and spiritual matters. He is a totally religious person."

The weekdays of the old archbishop were packed to the last degree. His days began at seven in the morning. From eight to eleven there was the early liturgy. Vladyko Luke gave a sermon every day. After the liturgy there was an extremely modest breakfast. At breakfast secretary Evgeniya Pavlovna Leykfeld would read two chapters of the Old and two chapters of the New Testament. Then the eparchial proceedings would start: patriarchal decrees, mail, appointments with the clergy, nominations and transfers, complaints of the authorities. The chancery was located right there in the apartment. The eparchial secretary, the elderly priest, father Vitaly, was used to the bishop requiring from him accurate reports and clear answers to questions. Archbishop Luke took decisions without delay and firmly.

The private secretary of vladyko Luke, Evgeniya Pavlovna Leykfeld, was very close to him. She was an intelligent elderly woman, a teacher of literature with a university education. With great diligence she took down hundreds of letters and sermons, and she wrote down (and repeatedly corrected with white correction fluid) the "Memoirs" [I.e., this autobiography (tr.)] of vladyko. During the time she worked for vladyko she read aloud the entire Bible four and a half times, and countless newspapers, magazines (some in German or French), theological treatises.

Reading printed media and books continued until lunch. After dinner some rest. Then from four to five, appointments with patients. Towards the evening a stroll on the boulevard along the shallow river Salhir. On his walk vladyko was often accompanied by his great-nephews Georgiy and Nikolai. Also here archbishop Luke does not lose time in vain: he relates the boys chapters from holy Scripture. After many years Georgiy and Nikolai Sidorkiny say they always remember these lessons, that were taught to them as if incidentally. And again office work: vladyko Luke would bend over sermons, letters, and surgical atlases until eleven in the evening.

Feast days are also very loaded for the bishop: "I write to you late in the evening. I just returned from Dzhankoy (from Simferopol to Dzhankoy it is a hundredkilometres), where I served on the day of the Protecting Veil of the most holy Mother of God. The Liturgy (and sermon) lasted for four hours and I blessed people for a whole hour. I am tired. I did not sleep all night," he wrote to Mikhail in 1951.

"Also my work is not small, especially now, during Lent. My service lasted for five hours. I get very tired..." As far back as Tambov some already grumbled, "What is this, a monastery, or what?" But vladyko Luke, however hard it was for him physically, served the full rule.

In the summers vladyko moved from the town to a small private dacha near Alushta. But here the same hard work continued day after day as well. The only difference was that on the southern coast of the Crimea he allowed himself somewhat longer walks and gladly swam in the sea.

Archimandrite Tikhon (Bogoslavets) was a spiritual friend and adviser of archbishop Luke. The archimandrite was deeply respected across the Crimea and the Ukraine, and people came to him from afar for spiritual guidance. Archimandrite Tikhon was the rector of the Crimean Inkerman cave monastery, and after it was closed he lived in Simferopol. There are testimonies of cases of ather Tikhon's extraordinary sagacity. Archimandrite Tikhon died in 1950. In a word spoken at a memorial service on an anniversary of the death of the starets, archbishop Luke said: "For more than three years, my first years in the Crimean eparchy, I had the good fortune to have him as a most intimate friend and a most valuable, dear advisor. I needed advice when there was severe discord, and such discord there was one after another in different places in our eparchy. All of his advice in church matters was not only wise, it was filled with the genuine spirit of Christianity. He gave me the kind of advice that can only be given by a true disciple of Christ." The memory of father Tikhon is honoured in the Crimea until now.

Archbishop Luke preached also to his family about Christ. The bishop wrote to his daughter Elena: "Do you and Anya (granddaughter) keep in mind your great responsibility before God to take care of teaching little Ira and Katyusha the law of God and prayers? You know they are exposed to the terrible danger of anti-religious propaganda. I could send you a patriarchal publication of the New Testament with a Psalter, if you and Anya promise me to read them to my great-granddaughters. With a lot of effort I managed to get four copies of the New Testament for all children." Vladyko Luke attested in one of his sermons, that at that time even some priests could not get a Bible.

The sons of vladyko became well-known scientists. Mikhail became an anatomist, a doctor of medicine, a professor. Valentin worked as an ophthalmologist and pathological anatomist, he was also professor, and a doctor of medicine. Alexey was one of the senior scientific collaborators and one of the founders of the I.M. Sechenov institute of evolutionary physiology and biochemistry, doctor of biological sciences.

Congratulating Mikhail on his name day, vladyko Luke wrote in a telegram: "...Martyr Mikhail, Prince of Chernigov, let him be an example of faithfulness to Christ for you."

When he was preaching the word of God archbishop Luke did not fear those who kill the body. When he delivered his first sermon in Tambov in February 1944, even the congregation was frightened. Father deacon Vasily Malin told that when people left the church that evening, many did not expect to ever hear or see their archpastor again. But at that time vladyko was not arrested, though the Tambov authorities repeatedly expressed their displeasure with the preacher.

In 1948 the Simferopol commissioner for orthodox church affairs reported to Moscow that archbishop Luke read a series of sermons with an anti-materialistic character in the cathedral.

In the mid-fifties Karpov spoke his mind about the sermons of the Crimean archbishop very sharply. When vladyko Luke complained that the Journal of the Moscow patriarchate did not publish his sermons, the chairman of the council for church affairs said: "There in the Simferopol cathedral you stir up mud, well, stir it up. But we will not let you publish in the international arena."

The bold sermons and actions of the archbishop frightened the unreligious medics, awakened concerns in the Crimean provincial committee, but at the same time they attracted the hearts of a great number of people to vladyko. Religious and unreligious patients spoke of him with love and gratitude.

Students, teachers, engineers and librarians went to church secretly. The head of the archaeological service of the Crimea, professor Paul Nikolayevich Schultz, a prominent scientist and a partisan in the war years, recalls how he and his wife came to the cathedral to hear the preaching of vladyko about the relationship between religion and science. For this he was summoned to the provincial committee. He was questioned, threatened, and deprived of a medal he deserved.

In the fifties, vladyko Luke and Schultz together tried to save a fourteenth century church from demolition. The church stood on the road from Simferopol to Stary Krym. The authorities declared that the church was in disrepair. At the request of the archbishop archaeologists inspected the building and found that the church could serve for two or three more centuries. Vladyko received the opinion of the experts and demanded right away that the church of ancient Christians be given to the Christians of the present, so that they could reestablish church services in it. The architectural monument, of course, was immediately pulled down for the bricks, and this story nearly cost professor Schultz his party-membership card. In the provincial committee they shouted at him: "A party-member and you help obscurantists! You resist the anti-religious propaganda?!"

In early 1951 archbishop Luke arrived by plane in Simferopol from Moscow where he had been on business. As a result of some misunderstanding there was no one to meet him at the airport. Vladyko was half-blind so he stood helplessly in front of the airport, not knowing how to get home. The townspeople knew him, helped him to take the bus. But the most amazing thing happened when archbishop Luke was going to get out at his bus-stop. At the request of the passengers the driver deviated from the route and drove three additional blocks; he brought the bus to a stop at the porch of the house on Hospital street. Vladyko got out of the bus to the applause of people who hardly used to go to church.

Even adherents of different creeds respected vladyko Luke. In particular the Jews, as sometimes happened in the lives of saints and righteous people. On major religious holidays the head of the Simferopol synagogue would come to congratulate the orthodox archbishop-physician. Vladyko Luke had once saved him from death. They even prayed for the orthodox archpastor in the synagogue, especially when they learned that he was ill. Vladyko Luke wrote to his son in 1957 that he had received congratulations from "the Moscow and Georgian patriarchs, from thirty bishops and from the Jewish community, which respects me for my kind attitude to Jews." Vladyko Luke began to lose his eyesight completely. His healthy eye began to see more poorly already in Tambov. In autumn 1947 the archbishop had to go to Odessa, to Filatov. The famous oculist examined vladyko for a long time and said he was still far from blindness. "Filatov found a clouding of the lens inside my eye that progresses slowly, and my ability to read will remain for a few years (from three to ten)," informed vladyko Luke.

Indeed, four years later, archbishop Luke could still read and write, though with difficulty. In the spring of 1952 vladyko overestimated his strength. He again spent a few weeks, as always from morning to evening, in the Moscow medical libraries. He overstrained his eye and his vision began to deteriorate every week. The sensation of colour vanished, objects turned into shadows. Now during visiting hours the professor had to ask the secretary the colour of a patient's swelling, what the patient's skin and mucous membranes looked like. In the end vladyko also gave up receiving patients and preparing the second edition of "regional anesthesia."

In the autumn of 1952 professor Filatov, who was in correspondence with vladyko Luke, offered him a preliminary operation: iridectomy. Vladyko did not agree because he was a diabetic, so the operation could end with purulence. People who were close to him grieved about him. Archbishop Luke learned to feel his way around the room. By touch he signed papers prepared by the secretaries.

The young bishop Mikhail Luzhskiy (Chub), who came to Simferopol to get acquainted with vladyko Luke, recalls:

I crossed the threshold and saw vladyko standing in the middle of the cabinet. His hands fumbled helplessly in the air, he was obviously trying to find the chair and desk he had lost. I said my name and I heard a low, firm voice, which was absolutely inconsistent with the posture of the master of the house: "How do you do, vladyko! I hear your voice, but I cannot see you. Come here, please." We embraced each other. Our conversation began. He was interested in my work for the church, and where I had studied, and who my teachers had been. During our talk, he got up and turned on a huge powerful lamp behind a clock with a transparent dial plate. He was clearly straining his eyes, but he made out the time himself. I also noticed further on that all he possibly could do, he did himself. His blindness had not undermined his will and it had not destroyed the brightness of his perception: when I asked him whether he sees dreams, vladyko replied, "Oh, and how! In colour!"

On vladyko Luke's name day, bishop Mikhail attended the festive moleben. He recalls that in the church the priests took the bishop by the arms, and when the moleben and the festive speeches were over, he walked out to the church porch by himself as if he had recovered his sight. At the exit a crowd of people was waiting for him with flowers: "For our dear doctor..." Vladyko was smiling as he stood there amidst those who had until recently been his patients. He blessed these children of his, as well as those who were in the church.

In 1954, after the July resolution of the central committee of the CPSU [communist party of the Soviet Union (tr.)] "On the improvement of scientific-atheist propaganda" a new wave of persecution of Christ's church began. Persecution and arrests of believers, public humiliation of priests, closing of churches, dispersal of "the public" on church holidays, reminded people of the older generation of the events of the twenties and thirties.

There is evidence that people who were in correspondence with vladyko Luke were persecuted. Engineer I.Y. Borisov was summoned to the Tambov KGB about his wife's correspondence with the Crimean archbishop Luke. The correspondence concerned purely religious and personal issues, but the engineer was told that if his wife Sofia Ivanovna did not cease to correspond with the churchman, he would be expelled from the Tambov boiler and machinery plant and nowhere in Tambov would he find himself a job. And his children, students, would be expelled from their institutes. Ilya Yakovlevich discerned on the table of the investigator a thick volume: "The case of Voyno-Yasenetsky," and in it he saw copies of letters from vladyko to Tambov and of letters from Sofia Ivanovna to Simferopol.

And in Simferopol, where the letters of the bishop were also opened and phone conversations were also bugged, a new position came into existence after the July resolution of the central committee: that of city church photographer. This person went around the churches every day and photographed the faces of parishioners. The weak in spirit who feared the persecutions ceased to appear in church, and those who were stronger appeared in a file of the corresponding government bodies for possible further investigations. In December 1954 in Simferopol a congress of priests of the Crimean eparchy took place. Archbishop Luke made a report in which he pointed out that of 58 churches in the Crimea only 49 had remained (the others were closed by the commissioner), and that two more churches were at risk. Vladyko Luke spoke openly about the fact that the propaganda, the covert and overt forms of pressure on believers did their job: the churches were empty. The ninth item on the agenda was formulated like this: "How did the anti-church propaganda affect the number of worshippers in churches." About the resolution of the central committee of the CPSU and Khrushchev's speech in newspapers the archbishop said briefly: "I did not find it necessary to refute these statements in the press. I limited myself to a sermon on the theme: 'Fear not, little flock.'" Even after two decades the Simferopol residents still remember this sermon on the day of the Protecting Veil of the most holy Mother of God in 1954:

... I know that the majority of you are very worried by the sudden intensification of anti-religious propaganda and you grieve... Do not worry, do not worry! This does not touch you. Tell me, please, do you remember the words of Christ from the Gospel of Luke: "Fear not, little flock; for it is your Father's good pleasure to give you the kingdom." (Lk. 12:32). Our Lord Jesus Christ spoke more than once about His little flock. His little flock had a beginning in His holy apostles. And then it multiplied and multiplied all the time... Atheism began to spread in all countries already, although especially in France later, in the early eighteenth century. But all and everywhere, despite the success of the popularization of atheism, a small flock of Christ is preserved, and it is preserved to this day. You, you, all of you who listen to me are this small flock.

And know and believe that the little flock of Christ is invincible, nothing can be done to it, it has nothing to fear, because it knows and always remembers the great words of Christ: "I will build My church; and the gates of hell shall not prevail against it." [Matt. 16:18 (tr.)] So, if even the gates of hell shall not prevail against His church, His little flock, then what should we be troubled about, worry about, grieve about? About nothing, nothing! The little flock of Christ, the authentic flock of Christ is invulnerable for any propaganda.

Thus spoke archbishop Luke less than four months after the head of state proclaimed it was necessary to finish off with the church once and for all. He spoke not in secret, but openly, in the church. And at that time he reassured many, strengthened many.

In early 1955 vladyko became completely blind. Soon after that the closest student of Filatov, teacher Shevelev came to the Crimea. Vladyko Luke wrote to a relative: "I firmly believe that the Lord will return my sight..." However, the ophthalmologist was at least two years too late. "Shevelev found I have far advanced glaucoma. The operation which he called 'risky' and 'very risky' would at best give me very little eyesight, but not at all the ability to read."

Long before losing his eyesight archbishop Luke wrote: "Prince Vasily Tyomniy [Vasily Tyomniy (the Blind) was Prince of Moscow from 1425-1462 (tr.)] said to the one who blinded him: 'You gave me a means to repent.'" After vladyko had lost his sight, no one heard him complain or grumble. "I took it as God's will that I was to be blind until death, and I took it calmly, even with gratitude to God." "My blindness I endure complacently and with full devotion to God's will," he wrote.

A year later archbishop Luke wrote to Aleksey: "Blindness is of course very hard, but for me, surrounded as I am by loving people, it is incomparably easier than for unfortunate solitary blind people, whom no one helps. For my episcopal activity blindness does not present a complete obstacle, and I think I will serve until death."

Imitating the holy archpastors, vladyko Luke tirelessly concerned himself with his herd. As before in the fifties, eparchial decrees of archbishop Luke exposed negligence and indifference, self-interest and disobedience. Shortly after the resolution of the central committee of the CPSU vladyko punished a whole number of priests who preferred a "light version" of baptism. He called one priest after another to Simferopol to personally verify whether the pastors did not make mistakes in the divine services. There *were* many mistakes, and vladyko Luke made this known in an epistle.

In "Exhortation to all priests of the Crimean eparchy" of 1955 the archbishop writes: "With great grief I heard and learned that many priests serve only on great feasts and Sundays. Services on Saturdays are very important. Priests who do not want to serve on those days when according to the statute polyeleos services and Saturday services are prescribed, usually excuse themselves by the fact that these services require unnecessary expenditures on candles, oil, wine, and especially by the fact that there is no one praying in the church..."

The archbishop met with new sorrows. The heavy struggle for churches with the commissioner for church affairs continued. An "engineering" protocol was fabricated to close the cathedral in Yevpatoriya: the building was unsafe, it was not suitable for exploitation. The commissioner sent a workers' brigade who dug around the foundation almost to the base, and allegedly some fault was found. Vladyko Luke started protesting, telegraphed to the patriarchate. Two engineers arrived and examined the cathedral, a new bill was drawn up: the foundation was completely safe and reliable. Nevertheless, the commissioner closed the cathedral, the local authorities quickly tore down the cupola and accommodated their offices and storerooms in the "unsafe" building.

Such lawlessness occurred frequently. Vladyko Luke sent his secretary to the commissioner with a protest, but the latter did not want to talk. The archbishop sent a complaint to the council for Russian orthodox church affairs, but Karpov sent a "commission" to Simferopol consisting of two cronies of the commissioner. Churches were closed also because of slanderous reports against priests and members of the clergy.

Vladyko wrote to his son in the summer of 1956, "...Church affairs are becoming heavier and heavier, churches are being closed one after the other, there are not enough priests, and the number of them is becoming less all the time." He repeatedly wrote to his son that he is "occupied to the extreme with most heavy and most unpleasant eparchial affairs." "The eparchial affairs are becoming harder all the time, in places it comes to open revolt against my episcopal authority. It is difficult for me to endure them with my eighty two and a halfyears. But I set my hopes on the help of God and continue to carry this heavy burden." "A member of the council for orthodox church affairs came to examine my claims to the commissioner, also this visit of his brought no good. I realized that my complaints will give little results."

A letter from 1960: "Church affairs are agonizing. Our commissioner is an evil enemy of Christ's church. He appropriates my episcopal rights more and more and he interferes with internal church affairs. He is completely wearing me out." "For over two months I had to fight with an exceptionally bad priest... The rebellion against my episcopal authority in Dzhankoy lasts since more than a year already. It is incited by the commissioner." "I have a lot more life-shortening experiences than you," says the bishop to his son. One long letter of vladyko is entirely devoted to clergy who "rebel against episcopal authority and do terrible things, they unlawfully obey the commissioner..."

In difficult times the love for vladyko Luke of people who respected him was particularly manifest. The famous physiologist, student and follower of I.P. Pavlov, L.A. Orbeli belonged to the number of scientists who honoured vladyko Luke. Aleksey Valentinovich Voyno-Yasenetsky recalls:

My conversation with Leon Abgarovich about my father occurred in August 1958. Orbeli already did not leave his bed at that time, and he died three months later. I will not undertake to reproduce our whole conversation, but I remember that it was surprising by its unexpectedness and sincerity. The point of Orbeli's words was to express his deep respect regarding my father, his admiration for the steadfastness of his convictions, for the fact that he was always a doctor of both body and spirit. The steadfastness and the unbending spirit of my father had to particularly impress Leon Abgarovich because he himself had not abandoned his scientific convictions in the years physiological science was devastated."

[As a result of the August session of the VASKhNIL (all-union Lenin academy of agricultural sciences) in 1948, three thousand biologists lost their jobs and many also their freedom. After that Stalin decided to organize a few more of such cleansing sessions. This was conceived in order to set at variance, to divide the scientific intelligentsia, to turn research institutions into nests of resentment, envy, vanity, and nationalist enmity.

In January 1950 the next terrible game of politics started in science: a joint session was held of the academy of medicine and the big academy. At this session a battle was announced "for the triumph of the physiological teachings of academician Pavlov." Part of the students of the great physiologist, academician Orbeli and his school were accused of misrepresentation, misunderstanding, disparagement of Pavlov's teachings. At this session Orbeli the first had heart trouble, which subsequently led him to the grave. "The low slander campaign against Orbeli so angered me that I wrote him a letter today," imparted vladyko Luke to his son Aleksey after the Pavlov session. (ed.)

Two months before Stalin's death the scientific community began preparations to declare Orbeli "enemy of the people" and to arrest him. Even then he courageously waited for this. Vladyko Luke wrote to L.A. Orbeli:

I am very touched by the fact that in the long conversation about me with my son Aleksey you asked him to pass me your sincere compliments as a scientist and a person... You know, of course, how difficult it was for me to swim against the turbulent current of rapid anti-religious propaganda, and how much torments it has caused me and causes me to this day...

I appreciate you very much as a very distinguished scientist and courageous fighter against unworthy scientists who hitch-hike on the glory of the great physiologist Pavlov.

May the lord God prolong your bright and highly useful life and may He facilitate the great workload of your diseased heart. I will pray to Him for this in my prayers.

Archbishop Luke, September 5th, 1958

During the administration of the Crimean eparchy his eminence Luke gave the greater part of his sermons. He began to preach in Tashkent, but because of his arrest and exiles he was forced to remain silent for many years. But since the spring of 1943 when the church in Krasnoyarsk was opened until the end of his life, archbishop Luke was preaching tirelessly. He wrote sermons, preached them, and then printed, corrected and circulated leaflets with the text, around the cities of the country. "I consider it my main episcopal duty to preach about Christ everywhere," he said in the Simferopol cathedral on October 31st, 1952.

In the thirty eight years he was a priest vladyko Luke gave twelve hundred and fifty sermons, of which not less than seven hundred and fifty were written down and put together in twelve thick typed volumes (about four thousand five hundred pages). The council of the Moscow theological academy called this collection of sermons "an exceptional phenomenon in the contemporary church and the theological life of the church" and the author was elected to be honourary member of the academy.

The Archbishop of Kuibyshev, Manuil wrote that the sermons of vladyko "are characterized by simplicity, sincerity, directness and originality." Considering a passage of his "Words on Good Friday," he says:

In the course of nineteen hundred years the best Christian preachers have spoken so much on this subject that it seems nothing new can be said anymore. And yet, the words of archbishop Luke are touching, like something unexpected: "The Lord took the Cross for the first time. He took the most terrible Cross. And after Him countless martyrs of Christ have taken on their shoulders their own crosses, smaller, but often also terrible crosses... Don't we also take on our cross and aren't we following Christ?" If you remember that these words were said in the spring of 1946, when his blindness was already approaching and archbishop Luke was forced to give up surgery, his humble willingness to take on a new heavy cross acquires a special meaning.

Archpriest Alexander Vetelev, professor of homiletics at the Moscow theological academy, knew vladyko Luke and was in correspondence with him. He believed the sermons were "a treasury of explanations of holy Scripture." "Every one of his sermons was breathing 'spirit and power.' By virtue of that they approach the glad tidings of the apostles and holy fathers. But also because of the strength of the sincere, deep feeling in them and their spirit of pastoral soul guardianship, and the simplicity and clarity of their content and presentation," wrote father Alexander [JMP, 1961, № 8, p. 37. (ed.)].

However, the apologetic work "Spirit. Soul. Body" of archbishop Luke is undoubtedly of interest from the point of view of science, but in the opinion of many orthodox theologians it is controversial from a dogmatic point of view.

During his administration of the Tambov and Crimean eparchies, remembers N.P. Puzin, archbishop Luke sometimes came to Moscow and served in various churches: "He loved to preach and considered preaching the most important thing in his episcopal ministry. I had to visit him sometimes in hotel 'Moscow' where he stayed, and I was sometimes present at services celebrated by him in different churches of the capital... I am happy that I was destined by fate to meet this remarkable man," wrote N.P. Puzin.

In the last years of his life vladyko Luke started to get very tired from services, sermons, eparchial affairs. At this time in the life of the Russian church sad and tragic events took place that deeply upset the old archbishop.

In the year 1960 a new wave of persecution of the church started in the country. A resolution of the central committee of the CPSU ensued. It said: "The leaders of some of the party organizations do not wage a persistent struggle against foreign ideology, they do not duly rebuff... idealistic religious ideology..." Numerous anti-religious articles, pamphlets and monographs appeared in print.

In March 1960 the council for orthodox church affairs presented the holy synod with a project of church-parish reform, which resulted in the bishops and parish priests being deprived of all authority. On July 18th 1961, already after the death of vladyko Luke, a council took place at which the change of the church statute was made.

Here is what vladyko wrote shortly before his death to a spiritual daughter of his: "I am wholly occupied and depressed by extremely important events in the Russian church. From all bishops a significant part of their rights will be taken away. From now on, the real masters of the church will be only church councils and twenty-people-parish-councils, of course, in alliance with commissioners. The higher and middle clergy only remain hired performers of church services. They will be deprived of the greater part of their authority to manage church buildings, property and money. You understand, of course, that now I cannot think about anything else..."

The death of the archbishop was approaching, he became pale, refused food, the heavy emotional experiences affected his condition. E.P. Leykfeld recalled: "The commissioner unspeakably tormented him by his persistently abusive actions against the church. He was a cruel man and completely unprincipled." "His last Liturgy he celebrated on Christmas, his last sermon he delivered on Forgiveness Sunday. He did not forget his duty to preach until the last minute, apparently he had prayed a lot..." wrote E.P. Leykfeld.

In the morning of June 11th, 1961, on the Sunday, when the memory of all the saints, resplendent in the Russian land is celebrated, archbishop Luke died.

"He did not grumble, he did not complain. He did not give any instructions. He passed away from us this morning at a quarter to seven. He breathed a little hard, then he sighed twice and once more hardly noticeably, and that was all..." wrote Evgeniya Pavlovna to vladyko's sister, V.F. Dzenkovich.

"His life went out at an advanced age after a prolonged illness that had gradually undermined his physical strength and that had prepared his spirit to an honourable, peaceful Christian death," wrote archpriest Alexander Vetelev in the obituary of the Journal of the Moscow patriarchate. "The death of his eminence Luke shocked not only his flock, but also all who knew him. It was an especially great loss for his flock. Because he had herded '...the congregation of God which...' he had, '...taking the oversight thereof, not by constraint, but willingly; not for filthy lucre, but of a ready mind; Neither as being lords over God's heritage, but being examples to the congregation' (1 Pet. 5:2-3)."

E.P. Leykfeld writes: "The funeral services followed one after another, the house was packed with people, people filled the yard, downstairs there was a huge line of people. The first night vladyko lay at home, the second in the Annunciation church, and the third in the cathedral. All the time the Gospel was read, only interrupted by funeral services. Priests relieved each other, and people kept coming and coming in a continuous file to bow down for vladyko... There were people from different districts, there were people who came from far away: from Melitopol, Genichesk, Skadovsk, Kherson. One group of people replaced another, and again silent tears flowed because there is no 'man of prayer' any more, now that 'our saint has left.' And then people remembered what vladyko had said, how he had cured, how he had comforted..." A heart had stopped beating, a heart that had been burning with a flame and active love for God and for people. Throughout the Crimea they spoke about the death of the archbishop. People shared details about his strict life, good deeds and the high moral demands he made to the faithful and the clergy. Even people who were far from the church understood that an outstanding personality had passed away. They understood this also on the Crimean provincial party committee, at the provincial KGB administration, and on the provincial executive committee. They had even prepared for the death of archbishop Luke in advance. In the night from the 10th to the 11th of June, when the provincial press had already started to print copies of the newspaper, an order followed to put in tomorrow's issue a big anti-religious article.

"... As soon as my father died, my brother Aleksey and I were invited to the city executive committee," recounts Mikhail Valentinovich Voyno-Yasenetsky. "It was explained that we would not be allowed to drive the body along the main street of Simferopol. Although the road from the cathedral by the main street is short, a funeral procession would hamper city traffic. Therefore, the route of the procession had been laid along streets on the outskirt. The city administration did not spare buses, they offered thirty of them, only so that a pedestrian procession would not form, only so that we brought father somewhat more quickly to the cemetery. We agreed... But everything turned out differently."

"The quiet of these solemn days," writes E.P. Leykfeld, "was broken by a terrible disturbance: there were negotiations with the commissioner who had banned the procession. He was convinced that if he allowed the procession six or seven old ladies would certainly be crushed ... But the parishioners and outsiders were all terribly outraged that the procession had been prohibited. One elderly Jew said: "Why don't they let people honour this righteous man?""

Archbishop Mikhail (Chub) came to the funeral of vladyko Luke on the instructions of the patriarchate. He also recalls the endless debates and negotiations over the grave of the Crimean archbishop. At first they forbade vladyko Mikhail to serve a burial service altogether. After a call to Moscow they allowed him to serve a burial service, but they brought forward the conditions under which the city authorities allowed to bury vladyko Luke. All accompanying people should go only on buses. A walking procession should not be created under any circumstances. To carry the coffin was out of the question. There should be no singing and no music at all. Quietly, quickly, unnoticeably, and in such a way that on June 13th at five in the evening, (not a minute later) the body of the archbishop was in the earth. In the evening after the negotiations in the building of the city executive committee, the chairman came again to Hospital street and again he talked endlessly about the rhythm of city life which may in no wise be broken, about how busy the main street is, etc.

Archbishop Mikhail performed the burial service of the deceased with an enormous confluence of believers. He concelebrated with almost all of the Crimean clergy.

"I made arrangements so that parting from vladyko could go on all night," remembers archbishop Mikhail, "and all night people came to the cathedral. The weather was hot and stuffy, but those who came to bid farewell did not seem to notice the stuffy heat. The people were crowded together in and around the cathedral day and night. At noon on the 13th, when we took the body of the deceased vladyko around the cathedral, the hearse stood already at the entrance, followed by a lorry that was filled to the brim with wreaths, then a passenger car for the archbishop, buses with relatives, the clergy, and choir members. There were still several buses for laymen who wished to participate in the burial, but no one wanted to sit in them. People made a close ring around the hearse. They clung to it with their hands, as if not wanting to let go of their bishop. For long the cars could not move from the churchyard. The commissioner ran steaming and hoarse from car to car, ran in and out of the buses, tried to persuade 'unnecessary and extraneous' people to step aside, not to interfere. No one listened. Finally, somehow they made some headway. Through the narrow streets of Simferopol the hearse and the buses could go at the speed the elderly women were walking. The three kilometers from the cathedral to the cemetery took us about three hours..."

Anna Dmitriyevna Stadnik, choir director at the Holy Trinity cathedral in Simferopol, tells:

When vladyko became very ill, already near his death, he said to his niece: "Will they allow singing 'Holy God' [the Trisagion (tr.)] for me?" And indeed, when he died, the authorities of the city of Simferopol fearfully armed themselves against there being any kind of solemn procession. People went to the cathedral... day and night to say goodbye to him, and day and night the priests read the Gospel. The day of the funeral came. We saw how the altar filled with people, they were talking about something with the priests, they gave some orders, demanded something. We felt in our hearts that something was going to happen.

And then came the time to take the body out of the church. Whilst singing "Holy God", we all went to the gate. Near the gate, on the left, there was a big empty bus. And when we came out of the gate and the hearse came to a halt, this bus moved and crossed our path. It wanted to completely cut us off from the hearse so that it would be driven off, and the people would be left behind, so that archbishop Luke would not be solemnly seen off. And then I shouted: "People, don't be afraid!" The women screamed in fear, because the bus was going to drive over them. I said: "Don't be afraid, people, it won't crush us, they won't go as far as that, grab the sides!" And then as many people as possible grasped the sides, they stuck to the hearse all around and the others followed them.

We walked perhaps a hundred metres. We had to turn to the main street, but the authorities did not want us to go that way, they again wanted to cut us off from the body and take it around the city, so that there wouldn't be any honour paid to the deceased. Here the women - no one gave them any order - hurled themselves on the ground before the wheels of the cars and said: "Only over our heads you will go to where you want." Then they promised us they would go the way we wanted. So we went down the main street of the city.

It was such a procession! It was full of people everywhere, the streets were jammed, and absolutely all traffic came to a stop. You can walk down this street in twenty minutes, but we walked for three and a half hours. There were people in the trees, on balconies, rooftops. This was something that had never happened before in Simferopol, and probably will never happen again, such a funeral, such respects!

Pharmacist Averchenko recalls: "It was a real demonstration. It seemed that the whole town attended the funeral: I remember the crowded balconies, people on rooftops, in the trees..."
And also E.P. Leykfeld remembers:
...The street was filled with women with white headscarves. Slowly, step by step, they walked in front of the car with the body of vladyko. Also the very old did not lag behind. There were three rows of outstretched hands and it was as if they were carrying this car. And up to the very cemetery the road was strewed with roses. And up to the very cemetery the crowd of white headscarves constantly sounded: "Holy God, Holy Mighty, Holy Immortal, have mercy on us..." Whatever they told this crowd, no matter how they tried to silence it, the answer was the same: "We bury our archbishop."
Vladyko Luke spiritually nourished the Crimean eparchy for more than fifteen years. His veneration has not come to an end at the present time. On the grave of archbishop Luke near the All Saints church people often come to pray, bring flowers, light candles. Many people have a lot of faith in the deceased archpastor: there are even known cases of healing at his grave. The last such incident occurred on June 24th, 1995: two broken ribs of a woman grew together.
Archimandrite Tikhon was a man who was spiritually close to vladyko Luke when he was alive. By the providence of God he rests near him also after his death: their graves are very close to each other. Father Tikhon was buried together with archbishop Gury (Karpov) (1815-1882), also an archpastor who was revered in the Crimea. His canonization is now being prepared. When the body of vladyko Gury was transferred to the All Saints cemetery, it turned out that it was incorrupt, and the following miracle happened: one hand that was damaged when transporting the body started bleeding. There are many cases of healing through the prayers of archbishop Gury.
The priests relate that the parishioners of the Crimean churches always enter the names of vladyko Gury, archimandrite Tikhon and vladyko Luke on the little lists given for the proskomedia [preparing the bread and wine for communion (tr.)] and on their synodicons [list with names of living and dead persons to remember (tr.)]. In all churches they pray for the repose of the souls of these deceased righteous hierarchs.

In the obituary placed in the "Journal of the Moscow patriarchate" (1961, № 8) the Russian church paid tribute to archbishop Luke like this:
Until the end of his days his soul remained alive, responsive, and charming. He gently loved people... And now his time of departure has come. He left us to stand before God and answer for himself and for his numerous flock. Living on earth he has "fought a good fight, finished [his] course, kept the faith" (II Tim. 4:7). Now in heaven, I dare hope, the Lord prepared for him "a crown of righteousness" as one "that love[d] His appearing" (II Tim. 4:8).
In one of his sermons the archpastor said:
You ask: "Lord, Lord! Is it really easy to be persecuted? Is it really easy to walk through the narrow gate and on the narrow rocky path?" You ask in bewilderment, so maybe in your heart has crept doubt whether the yoke of Christ is easy? And I'll tell you, "Yes, yes! It is easy, and extremely easy." Why is it easy? Why it is easy to follow Him on the thorny path? Because you will not go alone when you strain yourself to breaking point, and you will be accompanied by Christ Himself, because His boundless grace will renew your strength when you languish under His yoke, under His burden, because He Himself will support you and help you carry this burden, this cross.
I speak not from reason only, but I speak from personal experience, because I must testify that when I went a very painful path, when I was carrying Christ's terrible burden, it was not at all heavy, and this path was a joyous path, because I felt in actual fact, quite perceptibly, that next to me walks the Lord Jesus Christ Himself and He supports my burden and my cross. It was a tough burden, but I think of it as a luminous joy, as a great mercy of God. For God's grace is poured out abundantly over anyone who carries Christ's burden. Just because the burden of Christ is inseparable from the grace of Christ, just because if someone takes the cross and follows Him, He will not leave him all by himself, will not leave him without His help. He walks next to him, supports his cross, strengthens him with His grace.
Remember His holy words, for a great truth is contained in them. "...My yoke is easy, and My burden is light." All of you, all who believe in Him, Christ calls to follow Him, to take His

burden, His yoke. Fear ye not therefore. Go, go boldly. Do not be susceptible to the fears with which the devil terrifies you. They prevent you from going along this path. Spit at the devil, drive away the devil with the Cross of Christ, in His name. Raise your eyes to the mountain and you will see the Lord Jesus Christ, Who walks with you and lightens your yoke and burden. Amen. (Sermon of 28th January 1951: "Come unto Me, all ye that labor and are heavy laden.")

110   Archbishop Innokentiy (born Ivan Leoferov, 1890-1971). [tr.]

END AND THANKS GOD

www.ingramcontent.com/pod-product-compliance
Lightning Source LLC
LaVergne TN
LVHW041842070526
838199LV00045BA/1395